Some of the

MILITARY RECORDS OF AMERICA

(before 1900)

✳

Their Use and Value in
Genealogical and Historical Research

✳

"As it is the commendation of a good
huntsman to find game in a wild wood,
so it is no imputation if he hath not
caught all."—Plato

By

E. Kay Kirkham
Genealogist

Published By
DESERET BOOK COMPANY
Salt Lake City, Utah
1964

Printed by

DESERET NEWS PRESS

in the United States of America

INDEX

FOREWORD

The sole and single purpose of this book is to point out the genealogical and historical value of some of the more important military records of this country. The records that came about as a result of military service, pensions and bounty land warrants, are definitely treated on a limited scale. Without a doubt there are additionl records from military service, that have genealogical and historical value, that will not be mentioned or treated in this study. The subject of military records is one of the largest categories of records in our national history.

It is quite possible that criticism will come because of what has been left out of this book rather than what has been included in the book. A man in military service made a number of records other than pension records, bounty land warrants, muster rolls, etc. There is no doubt that the composite of all these many records would make a better genealogical, historical and military record but the scope of this book is limited to a treatise of a few of the better known records recognized for their genealogical and historical value.

My sincere thanks to my friends and professional co-workers in genealogy in Washington, D.C. whose encouragement has made this publication possible.

E. Kay Kirkham

INTRODUCTION

The importance of military records and their contribution to American genealogy cannot be over-emphasized. Experience has demonstrated that when a good American family genealogy is compiled it is done by consulting many sources of information. No one record in America can stand alone as *the one* record for the complete identification of the individual. The individual can be identified completely when *what he did* becomes a part of his individual self as much as his name and family. As the personality of an individual is a complete thing, so is the identity of that individual. In the past men have fought for God-given rights and freedom. This is our national heritage. The records that government agencies made as a result of their service to the country— is a vital part of our historical and genealogical heritage.

In Illinois a short time ago a county recorder made the statement to me that his vault contained all the records that had ever been made in that county. This statement was true only so far as the county recorders of the past were concerned. Perhaps the person who made the statement was not mindful of the fact that as the generations of the past have come and gone from his locality that they had gone to church, during their residence there as well as they had gone to the county court house for their legal business.

Perhaps also, the county recorder was unmindful that federal census enumerators had paid decennial visits to the county and had made a record of the people during their visit. Also, what about the men who had left the county to fight for home and country? Defense of the country was a national concern and the nation made the records for that man while he was absent from his home and the county seat. Then to supplement the county and national records we have the records made in the home of the individual. The composite of all the records cannot be more than the record of just who the individual was and what he did.

By deduction we can easily arrive at the conclusion that if one of the records that identifies the individual is lost or destroyed or cannot be located, then there is the probability that other records can be found about the individual. They need not be of necessity in the town, county seat or area in which he had lived.

As we will soon see military records are themselves somewhat of a composite record because recourse to other records about the individual was necessary in order to establish a claim for a pension or bounty land, etc. In the files of pension records and bounty land application files it is common indeed to find certified copies of marriage records, or the marriage certificate itself, or a page from the famly Bible and many other unusual records that identify the individual in one way or another. Also, historically, the things that he did are found in the files also.

A—THE VALUE OF MILITARY RECORDS

The Value of Military Records can be more clearly defined when we observe that verification and certification is required in order to qualify for the benefits, or bounties, of service. In fact, the file that seems to give the most information about an individual, his family, friends, military activities, residences, etc. is the record that is questioned, or disputed, for its authenticity. Large files, two and three folders an inch or more thick, will go into great detail to prove military service, fidelity or infidelity of a surviving widow, insanity and in one instance a total of sixty affidavits to support a claim that a veteran had "sore eyes" as a result of the Civil War.

As a more careful consideration is given to the pension and bounty land warrant application and declaration files it will be noted that the would-be beneficiary is attempting to qualify in one way or another under the provisions of some one particular Act of Congress. This is the essence of any one application. Later on the file will show other applications to qualify under another, and probably a more liberal act, until finally the applicant, his widow or heirs, will qualify. The pension and bounty land program of the government was not a static thing but was constantly undergoing changes, revisions, amendments and liberalizations, all seemingly to the benefit of the veteran.

Moreover, it is a fact that a wide variety of information is obtainable from the application files of widows and heirs of servicemen. A widow is required to prove her marriage to the soldier or to have affidavits from clergymen who married them, or supporting testimonials from relatives or friends as to the marriage.

The same is true within the application files of the heirs of soldiers. As a result of the information contributed, family records become more complete and the life stories of soldiers can be added upon. It is not possible to state the limits of information that might be found within a pension file. In consideration of all information, it must be remembered that the *object* of the file is to authenticate the qualification of the veteran under the provisions of the act. This is why, in some application files statements are found to prove that the veteran is necessitous—in dire need—of federal aid. It follows that some of the letters and testimonials (not witnessed or sworn to) were not acceptable to the Commissioner of Pensions as proof, nor might we acept them without verification.

The Historical Value of the files becomes evident when the applicant, or claimant, must recount his military service by naming his commanding officers, etc. to prove that he was in service. His service is subject to confirmation from government military service records. Unfortunately, many men served without regard to the small, but important, detail of being placed on a muster roll. Others served as scouts and spies for regiments and companies without having been oficially enrolled as a militia man. As a result of confirmation of military service there were many "rejected" pension applications. However, such pension applications will contain considerable genealogical information.

As recounts are made by the veteran serviceman, the history of an engagement is forever retained within the lives of the people who lived through it. Officially, the records lacked the color, drama and imagination as given to them by the combat soldier—who survived. The files remind us that wars have been fought, not only under arduous conditions but by troops who over-ran the crops of the fields, the thresholds of homes—and left indelible memories upon the hearts and minds of the men who faced the enemy, the veterans. It is a pitiful thing to read of a re-told story from a veteran who has lost his clear-cut memory, his discharge papers, his buddies in arms and "no one is now living who can confirm his battle record."

An "abstract" of a file may give but little information. Actually, there is no substitute for a complete examination of the file by one who not only knows the information he is looking for but where he expects to find it.

B—THE AGENCIES DEFINED

The *Veterans Administration*, Washington 25, D.C. has records based on service in World War I and II and the Korean War. This agency is not under the War Department and does not have the same restrictions as enforced by the War Department.

The *Adjutant General's Office* (AGO) as defined in the *Preliminary Inventory of the Records of the Adjutant General's Office* #17, 1949, page 1.

"The Adjutant General's Office is, then, esentially one handling records, orders and correspondence of the Army. To it finally come for custody practically all records concerned with the Military Establishment, including personnel of the Army, both Regular and Volunteer, together with large bodies of other records representing discontinued commands, special collections and non-currant holdings of bureaus of the War Department. The records representing the central correspondence of the Office constitute one continuous series of files from 1800 to date.

(page 2) ". . . the record keeping of the Office falls into three distinct periods, designated as follows: (1) the "Book Period", 1800 to 1889 during which incoming correspondence was maintained in a letters received file, after being entered in registers of letters received, and outgoing correspondence was copied in letters sent volumes; (2) the "Record Card Period", 1890-1917, during which the information . . . was copied on cards and (with other information) to form what was known as the 'document file'. (3) The Decimal Classification Period", beginning in 1917."

The *War Department* Revolutionary War records are defined and inventoried in the National Archives and Records Service (General Services Administration) Publication, *"War Department Collection of Revolutionary War Records, Preliminary Inventory* #144, compiled by Mabel E. Deutrich, Washington, 1962.

The National Archives is a repository for many of our military records. In 1948 a *Guide to the Records in the National* Archives was issued and there have been a number of supplemental accession lists since that time. Also, the National Archives and Records Service (GSA) Washington 25, D.C. has issued several pamphlets of helpful information to genealogical and historical research.

The National Archives, Washington, D.C., Publication #61-14, general information.

Age and Citizenship Records in the National Archives, Publication #61-13.

Compiled Military Service Records in the National Archives, Publication #63-3.

Pension and Bounty Land Warrant Files in the National Archives, Pub. #60-9.

Records in the National Archives Relating to Confederate Soldiers, #60-10.

Genealogical Records in the National Archives, publication #62-1.

Genealogical Sources Outside the National Archives, publication #62-7.

Also available:

List of National Archives Microfilm Publications, 1961, publication #61-12.

The above pamphlets and the microfilm publication are to be ordered from the Publications and Exhibits Branch, Room G-10, National Archives, Washington 25, D.C. There is no charge for the publications above.

The General Services Administration, National Archives and Records Service, National Archives Building, Washington 25, D.C. performs a public service in providing copies of certain of their records. Their form, Na - 288, *order for photocopies concerning veteran* is quoted as follows:

"Fill out this form as fully as you can. As we often have files for several different veterans of the same name, the more information we have, the quicker and surer will be our recognition of the correct file.

"Use a separate form for each veteran.

"Enclose one dollar, preferably a money order or check payagle to *General Services Administration* (as above).

"Some years ago, in order to reduce the cost of our services and to decrease the likelihood of copying errors, we discoutinned the practice of transcribing genealogical information from the records and adopted, instead, the practice of furnishing photocopies of the original documents for a fee. This practice has proved, on the whole, satisfactory to our patrons.

"Now, in order to reduce the average amount of fees and to speed up our service, we have installed a flat fee system.

"Please use the reverse of this form to order photocopies of records relating to a person who served in the United States or Confederate Armed Forces. We can furnish photocopies relating to the following subjects:

    a. United States military service before World War I and Confederate military service.

    b. United States (not Confederate or State) pensions claimed on the basis of service before World War I, and

    c. United States (not State) bounty lands claimed on the basis of service before 1856.

"Send us the completed form with one dollar. If you send more than one form at one time, your remittance should be as many dollars as you send forms. Each order will be handled separately; so you may not receive all your photocopies at the same time. Be sure to enter your name and address on each form.

"If we find a file for the person identified by your order, we will send photocopies of the documents we think most likely to be of interest to you. If we do not find a file that we can identify with the person in whom you are interested, we will refund your money."

Note: Inplacing orders for copies of records be sure to state the kind of record that you are interested in whether it be a military *service* record or military *pension* record.

C—DEFINITION OF BASIC RECORDS

Throughout the techincal treatise of the subject of pensions and military service records, frequent reference will be made to the book by Dr. William Henry Glasson, published by the Oxford University Press, New York, 1918, Carnegie Endowment for International Peace. Dr. Glasson's explanation of the word pension:

"A military pension is a regular payment made by a government to one who has served in its armed forces, or to his widows or dependent relatives. It is a gratuity given to former soldiers or their relatives for reasons satisfactory to the government, whether as compensation for physical injuries, or to relieve want, or purely as a reward. Army pay and pensions are not matters of contract. No claim for a pension can be enforced against the State. In the performance of his duty, a soldier may become the victim of wounds, casualties or disease, but these incidents of warfare give him no right to a pension enforceable against an unwilling government.

"Pensions that have been granted to our former soldiers may be divided into *invalid pensions* (or disability pensions) and *service pensions.* An invalid pension is one granted to a soldier on account of wounds or injuries or disease contracted in military service. *A Service Pension* is granted in recognition of military service for a specified length of time, whether a few weeks or months or many years."

In the explanations that will follow particular attention should be given to whether the text discussion is about *pensions* or about *Military Service,* or military service pensions. It is to be remembered that the *War Department* kept its own records in its own way and made indexes for them which covered different periods of years than did those indexes that pertained to pensions as such. While the explanations will be made in the text, the reader should be alerted constantly to this fact. Service records and pension records are different not only in their source as a record but in their genealogical content.

From the book, *Preliminary Inventory of the Records of the Adjutant General's Office,* #17, Washington: 1949, the following definitions of value in research: "The history and records of the *Record and Pension Office* are closely interwoven with those of the *Adjutant General's Office.* Formed by a combination of a division of the Surgeon General's Office, this unit existed separately from 1889 to 1904, when, as noted above, it was combined with the *Adjutant General's Office,* to form the Military Secretary's Office, which in 1907 became the "Adjutant General's Office." The Record and Pension Office records obtained by this combination now form an integral part of the records of the Adjutant General's Office and are described in this inventory. They are highly significant for historical research and for information concerning the military service of individuals who fought in the wars from the Revolution through the Spanish-American War."

(Page 17) *"Muster Rolls,* 1784-1912—A muster roll is a list of all troups actually present on parade or otherwise accounted for, made on the day of muster or review of troops under arms in order to take account of their number, inspect their arms and accoutrements, and examine their condition . . . There are several types of muster rolls, including descriptive rolls, muster-in and muster-out rolls (for volunteers only) and the regular muster-for-pay rolls for individuals detatchments, companies and regiments and for field, staff and band.

"A regular muster-for-pay roll includes the names of the personnel of the organization, with names of commissioned officers and noncommissioned officers coming first, followed by names of privates in alphabetical order; the date and place of joining service; by whom enrolled and for what period; the date of muster into service; the date of last pay and for what period, together with the amount received and remarks . . . which include absentees, desertions and deaths. Muster and descriptive rolls give additional information, including place of birth; age at date of muster; previous occupation; color of hair, eyes and complexion; bounty paid and amounts due and . . . remarks.

Perhaps additional explanation is needed to distinguish between *Military Service Record* and *Pension* records. From the National Archives and Records Service publication, "Compiled Military Service Records in the National Archives" publication #63-3, we have the following:

"Description of the records—a compiled military record is kept in a jacket envelope filed with those for other soldiers who fought in the same war and regiment or similar unit. The record consists of (1) one or more card abstracts of entries relating to the soldier as found in original rolls, returns, registers or other records; (2) sometimes documents . . . pertaining solely to the particular soldier. The card abstracts of service—if complete— may serve to trace that service from beginning to end, but normally to little more than account for where he was at a given time." The only information of genealogical interest that they are likely to give is his age and place of enlistment.

Note: Historically these cards serve the purpose of the history of campaigns.

The contents of pension files as such, are commented upon in several places in this book, examples from the various wars are given, etc.

Note: (II ed.) The National Archives has issued a current publication entitled—"A Guide to the Genealogical Records of the National Archives" NARS-GSA #64-8-50c. This excellent and needed book gives good detail regarding Military Records in the National Archives.

BOUNTY LANDS

Other than pensions, bounty land records probably give more information than any other type of record that arises from military service. At the National Archives there is a general index to bounty lands, and while some of the bounty land files have been included in the pension files, this index should still be consulted for the probability of records arising from military service.

To more adequately describe the provisions of the various Bounty Land Acts the following information is taken from the book, *Army and Navy Pension Laws, and Bounty Land Laws of the United States*, including sundry resolutions of Congress from 1776 to 1854 inclusive. Compiled by Robert Mayo, M.D. and Ferdinand Moulton, Counsellor at Law, II ed., Baltimore, Lucas Bros, 1854.

(Page xxx) "The general subject of land bounties may be subdivided under the following heads, viz.:

I. Bounty lands granted for Revolutionary services and their considerations connected with the Revolutionary War.

II. Bounty land granted to non-commissioned officers and soldiers for services in the War of 1812, in consideration of enlistments for five years, or during the war; including Canadian refugees, provided for after the war.

III. Bounty lands granted to non-commissioned officers, musicians, marines, etc. who served in the Mexican War.

IV. Bounty lands granted for services in various Indian Wars from the year 1790 and for services in the second and third foregoing heads.

I *For Revolutionary Service.* . . . by the resolution of 14 August 1776 in retaliation of the invitation and compulsory measures of the British Government to induce our troops to desert our service, it was promised and promulgated, "that all foreigners who shall leave the service of His Britannic Majesty in America and become members of any of these States, shall be prohibited in the free exercise of the rights, privileges and immunities of the native citizens thereof, as shall leave the armies of His Britannic Majesty in America, and become citizens of these States, unappropriated lands in the following quantities and proportions, viz.:

To a Colonel ....1,000 acres
To a Lieutenant Colonel 800
To a Major 600
To a Captain 400
To a Lieutenant 300
To an Ensign 200
To a non-commissioned and to all others
    in proportion 100

". . . and in pursuance of the resolutions of 23 April 1783 and the 7 Apr. 1798 lands were granted to Canadian and Nova Scotia refugees, distinguished into several classes, in the following proportions, viz.: (a) to those of the first class, not exceeding 1,000 acres; (b) to those of the intermediate classes, according to prescribed rules. (c) to those of the last class, not exceeding 100 acres.

". . . Under the several resolutions refferred to below, officers and soldiers of the U.S. who served to the end of the war, were entitled to land bounty and of those who never received the bounty during their lives their representatives are entitled according to the subjoined rates (list of resolutions noted)

To a Major General	1,100 acres
To a Brigadier General	850
To a Colonel	500
To a Lieutenant Colonel	450
To a Major	400
To a Captain	300
To a Lieutenant	200
To an Ensign	150
To a non-commissioned Officer	100
To a soldier	100

To the director of the medical department, 850 acres; to the Chief Physician and Purveyor, 500 acres; to Physicians, Surgeons and apothecaries 450 acres; to regimental surgeons and assistants, 400 acres; to hospital and regimental surgeon mates, 300 acres.

II For the War of 1812 ". . . five years service, or during the war, etc. by the Act of 24 December 1811 . . . each of the non-commissioned officers, musicians and privates, who enlisted for five years, or for during the war and were honorably discharged and heirs of those who died or were killed whilst in the service, were promised land bounty of one hundred and sixty acres.

". . . by the Act of 6 Feb. 1812 . . . for certain volunteer corps for twelve months . . . 160 acres (later not honored by the government). Under the Act of December 1814, a double bounty of 320 acres was promised . . . to those who would enlist and serve in conformity with the provisions of the Act.

". . . by the Act of the 5th March 1816, for granting bounties in land extra pay to certain Canadian volunteers, the said volunteers were entitled to land in the following proportions, viz.: To each Colonel, 960 acres, to each Major, 800 acres, to each Captain, 640 acres; to each subaltern officer, 480 acres; to each non-commissioned officer, musician and private, 320 acres. Also to the medical and other staff, the like proprotions, according to their rank. (Later the Act of 3 March 1817 changed the above bounties to one-half.)

III For Service in the War with Mexico.

"By the 9th section of the Act of 11 February 1847, "raising for a limited time an additional military force" 160 acres of land, or in lieu of the scrip of $100, bearing interest, was promised . . . to non-commissioned officers, musicians and privates, who should enlist in the regular army, or volunteer corps, to serve with the War with Mexico. (additions and variations noted later in this Act.)

IV For services in various Indian Wars since 1790, the War of 1812, and in the War with Mexico.

"The Act of 28 September 1850, provides bounty lands for commissioned officers, etc. who served in the War of 1812 and in the War with Mexico . . . at the rate of 160 acres or 40 acres according to their respective period of service from 1-9 months.

* * *

The records of our wars have spanned one hundred and eighty-six years, almost two centuries, and it is to be expected that the nature of records changed just as much as the methods of making war have changed. Also, the vocabulary of a hundred and eighty-six years ago is not the same as it is today. Thus it is necessary to review the acts for pensions and bounty lands as well as provide a short glossary of military terms in the appendix of this book. The need for this study became apparent when the historical and genealogical value of the records was evident and the need for better understanding of them was long over-due.

Bounty Land application by an "heir"
of soldier, War of 1812. Page -1-

The State of Ohio
County of Trumbull, ss

On this eleventh day of
July AD one thousand eight hundred and fifty one personally
appeared before me, David D Belden a Notary Public
within and for said County, Nicholas Mizner aged about
forty years a resident of Brookfield said County, who being
duly sworn according to law says, that he is the duly
appointed Guardian of Rhoda Mizner of Vernon said
County, as appears by the Certified Copy of his Letters of
Guardianship hereto attached, that said Rhoda Mizner, is
the only surviving minor child of James Mizner, the
Brother of this deponent, who died at Dillsborough in the
State of Indiana on or about the   day of
September AD 1839 that said James Mizner left a
widow Elizabeth Mizner, who also died at said
Vernon aforesaid, on the   day of June AD 1846
& that said Minor was born on the   day of July
AD 1835 — And that said Rhoda Mizner is now aged
sixteen years —

    This deponent further says, that
he was present at the time the said Elizabeth Mizner
was buried, that he has heard the said Elizabeth say,
in her life time that she has been at the grave of her said
deceased Husband, having gone to Indiana to settle
the Expenses of his last sickness — The said James if now living would be

... years old This deponent also says, that he has been often informed and believes the fact to be, that the said James Wynne was the identical James Wynne who was a Private in the Company Commanded by Captain Asa Hutchins, in the 5 Regiment of Ohio Militia Commanded by Col Richard Hays in the war with Great Britain declared by the United States on the 18th day of June 1812, that said James was drafted at Hubbard said County of Trumbull, on or about the twenty fifth day of August AD 1812 for the Term of three Months, that he was in actual service in said war for about three months, and was discharged on account of sickness.

He makes this declaration for the purpose of obtaining the bounty Land to which the said Rhoda may be entitled under the act granting bounty land to Certain officers, and soldiers who have been engaged in the military service of the United States, passed September 28th 1850 —

Nicholas Wynne

Sworn to and subscribed before me the day and year above written firstly, —

David D. Belden
Notary Public

BOUNTY LAND, ACT OF 1855.

WIDOW'S APPLICATION FOR FIRST WARRANT.

——•·◄►·•——

Note: widow states that she has n[o] record of marriage. Therefore the affidavit on following page was required as a substitute.

STATE OF CONNECTICUT, } ss: *East Haddam*
COUNTY OF *Middlesex*

On this *30th* day of *March* A. D. one thousand eight hundred and *55* personally appeared before me, a *Notary Public* within and for the county and State aforesaid, *Margaret Gladding* aged *75* years, a resident of *Haddam* in the State of Connecticut, who, being duly sworn according to law, declares that she is the widow of *James Gladding*, deceased, who was a *Corporal* in the company commanded by ~~Captain~~ *Lieutenant Aaron Brainard* in the *7th* regiment of *Infantry* commanded by *Colonel Brainard*, in the war with Great Britain, declared by the United States on the 18th day of June, A. D. 1812, *Connecticut Militia.*

That her said husband *was drafted* at *Haddam* on or about the *30th* day of *April* A. D. 18*14*, for the term of *One month*, and continued in actual service in said war for the term of *21 days*, and was honorably discharged at *Say Brook* on the *20th* day of *May* A. D. *1814. That his discharge is lost.*

She further states that she was married to the said *James Gladding* in *Say Brook* on the *first* day of *January* A. D. 17*97*, by one *Richard Ely*, a *Minister* and that her name before her said marriage was *Margaret Tripp*; that her said husband died at *Haddam* on the *12* day of *October* A. D. 18*50* and that she is now a widow. *and has no record of marriage. And has never before made application for or received Bounty Land under this or any [act] of Congress* She makes this declaration for the purpose of obtaining the bounty land to which she may be entitled under the act approved March 3, 1855.

................*Margaret Gladding*............

We, *James Gladwin & Laura Gladwin* Both residents of *East Haddam* in the State of Connecticut, do upon our oaths, declare that the foregoing declaration was signed and acknowledged by *Margaret Gladding* in our presence, and that we believe, from the appearance and statements of the applicant, that she is the identical person she represents herself to be.

................*James Gladwin*............

................*Laura Gladwin*............

Affidavit to marriage of widow's
application for bounty land. See
previous page for declaration

State of Connecticut }
County of Middlesex } SS East Haddam.

On this fifth of April AD 1855. Before the subscriber a Notary Public within and for the county and State aforesaid, duly authorized by law to administer Oaths Personally appeared Gideon Higgins aged 72 years and Austin S. Shaler aged 50 Years Both, residents of East Haddam in the State of Connecticut and county of Middlesex. Who being duly Sworn according to Law, do each for themselves. Depose & say. That Margaret Gladding who makes the accompanying declaration is the widow of James Gladding late of Haddam. who is now deceased who was, reputed to be a Corporal in Lieutenant Aaron Brainards company of Connecticut Militia in the War of 1812, with England. That they knew said James Gladding & said Margaret Gladding lived together as husband and wife and raised a large family of Children. and said James Gladding always treated said Margaret Gladding as his lawful wife and were so considered by the community where they lived: and Deponents verily believe them to have been married on the first day of January 1797 as set forth in the accompanying Declaration. That said James Gladding died on or about the second day of October AD 1850. and that said Margaret Gladding is now a widow. and that they have no interest in said claim.

Gideon Higgins

Austin S. Shaler

Sworn to and and subscribed on the day & year first above written before me & I certify that Gideon Higgins & Austin S. Shaler are credible witnesses. That the words "reputed to be a" were inserted by me, before administering the oath & that I have no interest in this claim,

Wm. H. Buell
Notary Public

CHAPTER I

COLONIAL WARS

A—Dates and names of Wars

King William's War—1690 to 1697—between England and France.
Queen Anne's War—1702-1713.
King George's War—1744-1748—between England and France.
King Philip's War 1675-1676—In New England between Indians and the English.

French and Indian War — 1754-1763 — The first fighting took place in America before the war was formally declared in Europe. In 1749 a French expedition under Celoron de Bienville took formal possession of the Ohio Valley. In 1754 Duquesne, Governor of Canada, sent an expedition to build a series of forts and roads into this same territory. In behalf of Breat Britain and Virginia, which claimed this area, Governor Dinwiddie, of Virginia, sent George Washington, a young man of twenty-one, to demand that the French vacate. In refusing, the French built the Fort Duquesne on the present site of Pittsburg, considered then to be the key to the Ohio Valley.

In 1755 General Braddock arrived in America with an army of British regulars. In 1759 the Battle of Quebec was fought. This was the defeat of the French general Montcalm by the British General Wolfe. This battle decided the ultimate fate of New France in America. Although the French and Indian War (between Great Britain and France) started in 1754 in America the British formally declared war on France the 18 May

1756. This was was fought both in America and Europe. In Europe it was known as the "Seven Years War". The was ended in 1763 by the signing of the Peace of Paris. In the peace treaty of 1763 France surrendered to Great Britain all of her possessions on this continent east of the Mississippi River, except the City of New Orleans.

B—Bounties received

(Source: "Military Pension Legislation in the United States by William Henry Glasson, PhD. N.Y. Columbia University Press, 1900. Vol. XII #3 of series Studies in History, Economics and Public Law.)

(Page 12) "Many of the English colonies in America had provided for the relief and maintenance of wounded and maimed soldiers. . . . in 1636 the Pilgrims at Plymouth enacted in their court that any man who should be sent forth as a soldier and returned maimed should be maintained competently by the colony during his life. (Ply. Col. Rec. XI, Laws, 106)

"As early as 1644 the Virginia Aseembly passed a disability pension law, and later provided for the relief of the indigent families of the colonies soldiers who should be slain. (Hening's Statutes at Large, i, 287, ii, 331, 347, 440.) We find similar acts among the colonial statutes of Maryland and New York during the later part of the 17th century.

"In 1718 Rhode Island enacted a remarkably comprehensive pension law.

". . . nor during the Revolution did the States rely entirely on Congress to take the initiative in granting pensions. Some of them, notably Virginia and Pennsylvania, independently promised liberal allowances to their disabled soldiers. . . . this early national law (of August 26, 1776) agreed in principle with the colonial disability provisions which we have already considered. It aimed to encourage enlistment in the Revolutionary Army."

(Source: *Dictionary of American History* by James Truslow Adams, editor, 1940, N.Y. Scribner's and Sons.)

Bounties—Military—"When war forces were raised by volunteering instead of conscription of militia obligations, bounties stimulated recruiting. For Indian and French campaigns, colonies offered cash inducements, sometimes solely to induce enlistments, sometimes for bringing clothing or weapons into service."

Land grants were given to veterans of the French and Indian War by order of the King of England. At least part of these bounty lands were in the present State of New York. Several of the better American History books available have maps and explanations regarding these bounty lands and where they are located, especially in New York State.

C—Location and Availability of Records

Several of the States have published their colonial records, at least those records that have been retained by the States from the time when they were colonies. Among these States are North Carolina, Pennsylvania, Georgia and possibly others.

It is not known to the author the extent and availability of the records of colonial militia or mercenaries as made and maintained by the British Government. There is at least one publication of British records not available in our original archives here in America. There might be others available in England or in State archives in this country.

CHAPTER II

THE PERIOD OF THE REVOLUTIONARY WAR
1776-1811

The Revolutionary War started in Massachusetts 19 April 1775. The Declaration of Independence was at Philadelphia, Pa., 4 July 1776. General Cornwallis surrendered at Yorktown, Va., 19 October 1781. Peace treaty was signed in 1783. Of the thirteen original States the following were known as slave states: Deleware, Maryland, Virginia, North Carolina, South Carolina, Georgia; free states: New Hampshire, Massachusetts, Rhode Island, Connecticut, New York, New Jersey, Pennsylvania.

A—*Provisions of some of the various Acts of Congress.*

(Source: *Federal Military Pensions* in the United States, by William Henry Glasson, Ph.D., Oxford University Press, N.Y., 1918.)

Page 20 "With the outbreak of hostilities Congress was petitioned for help and redress to those who had suffered as a result of the war. A committee was appointed to consider proposals for the wounded and disabled. The plan submitted by this committee was adopted by Congress August 26, 1776 and became the first national pension law in the United States. Among other provisions the law promised half pay for life or during disability to every officer, soldier or sailor losing a limb in any engagement or being so disabled in the service of the United States as to render him incapable of earning a livelihood.

Page 21 "On September 25, 1778 Congress again delt with the matter of invalid pensions and extended relief to those who had been disabled before 26 Aug. 1776 and since the commencement of hostilities, April 19, 1775.

Page 21 "During the progress of the War further provisions for invalids were made by the Act of April 23, 1782.

Page 22 "The final resolutions of the Congress of Confederation on the subject of invalid pensions were passed on June 11, 1788 . . . This was amended later in 1792 and at the time there were 1,500 invalid pensioners on the rolls.

Page 33 ". . . after many attempts by George Washington in particular, the Congress could not yet be persuaded to promise half-pay for life to officers. But on August 24, 1780 the report . . . was again taken up and favorable consideration was given to the claims of the widows and orphans of officers. In 1788 Congress had promised seven years half-pay to officers serving to the end of the war. Now a resolution was adopted granting half-pay for the same length of time to the widows of those officers who had died, or should die thereafter, in the service. If there was no widow surviving, or in case of her death or remarriage, the half-pay was to go to any orphan children of the deceased. This in substance was the first national pension for the benefit of widows and orphans.

Page 50 *Commutation Certificates* were given to officers (2,480) for service in the Revolutionary War but delayed redemption of them and delayed payment of accrued interest, failed to relieve the need of the officers. When most of the survivors of the Revolutionary War were aged seventy or older . . . President John Quincy Adams, in his message of December 1827 recommended to the consideration of Congress "the debt rather of injustice than gratitude to the surviving warriors of the Revolutionary War" Congress passed the law of 15 May 1828.

Page 51 "The Act of 1828 granted full pay for life beginning with March 3, 1826, to the surviving Revolutionary War officers in the Continental Line, who had been entitled to half-pay for life by the resolution of Oct. 21, 1780.

Page 62 "A number of minor changes in pension laws were enacted between 1800 and 1828.

Page 67 "The Law of 1818 . . . provided that every person who had served in the Revolutionary War to its close, of for the term of nine months or longer at any period of the war, on the continental establishment or in the navy, and who was a resident citizen of the United States, and was by reason of his reduced circumstances in life "in need of assistance from his country for support", should receive a pension. The administration of the law was taken before the district judges of the United States or before any court of record of the state or county in whcih the applicant resided.

Page 71 "Abuses of the pension laws caused a new law to be written in 1820 under which many were stricken from the (pension) rolls.

Page 80 "A new pension bill became law in 1832 which took the form of an extension to additional survivors of the Revolutionary Army of the full pay for life which had been granted by the Act of May 15, 1828 . . . under provisions of the new law, the Secretary of War reported that 24,260 persons applied for benefits therefrom . . .

Page 93 "After the service pension Act of 1832, there were but few minor provisions for the benefit of Revolutionary soldiers. By Jun. 30, 1867 all the Revolutionary soldiers on the pension rolls had died, however during the following years two others were pensioned and Daniel F. Bakeman the last survivor died on April 15,

1869, age 109. In 1869 . . . there were 887 Revolutionary War widows on the pension list . . . in 1906, 123 years after the close of the Revolutionary War one widow was still on the pension list.

Page 94 "(A summary) "From the invalid-pension resolution of August 1776, to the last provision for widows in March 1878, there was over a century of Revolutionary pension legislation. First invalid-pension laws were passed for the benefit of officers and privates. Service-pensions of half-pay for life were promised to officers who served until the end of the war, but on account of bitter opposition, the officers received instead of half-pay a gross sum in commutation certificates. In 1818 a precedent was established for service-pensions to volunteer armies by the grant of such pensions to the indigent veterans of the Revolution. A more liberal law was passed in 1832, and service pensions were granted to the Revolutionary War soldiers regardless in income or property. The widows of Revolutionary soldiers (with the exception of widows of officers) received no pension until 1836. As death decreased the number of survivors on the pension roll the laws for the benefit of widows were from time to time made more comprehensive.

"Estimates on the total of Revolutionary War soldiers granted pensions—in 1874 the Commissioner of Pensions reported 20,485 Revolutionary soldiers pensioned under the Act of 1818; 1,200 under the Act of May 15, 1828 and 33,425 under the Act of 1832 or total 55,110.

Page 95 "Elsewhere in the same report the number of Revolutionary service pensions is given as 57,623 (including duplications). Thousands who were pensioned under the Act of 1818 were dropped from the rolls because they were not indigent. The number of original soldiers and sailors claims allowed on account of the

Revolutionary War as given in the report of the Commissioner of Pensions in 1915 was 52,504.

Page 98 "Pension provisions for the regular army included in the Act of 30 April 1790.

Page 99 "In the United States the retirement system for the officers and enlisted men of the regular army has not been ordinarily treated as a part of the national military pension system."

★

REVOLUTIONARY WAR PERIOD

B—*Bounties received*

Note: on page xix in the Introduction a treatise is given on the bounty lands for the Revolutionary War and other wars.

Source: *Dictionary of American History*, by James Truslow Adams, ed. 1940, N.Y. Scribner's and Sons. Quoted as follows:

"When war forces were raised by volunteering instead of conscription or militia obligations, bounties stimulated recruiting. For the Indian and French campaigns, colonies offered cash inducements, sometimes solely to induce enlistments, sometimes for bringing clothing or weapons into service. The practice was adopted during the Revolutionary War by both Congress and the States. In January 1776, $6.2/3 was offered to fill the Canadian expedition. In June $10. for 3 years enrollments 'for the war'. To fill militia quotas States offered their own bounties, so that States and Congress bid against one another. . ."

C—*Availability and Use of Records*

As to the availability of records at the National Archives it is suggested that you avail yourself of the free literature as listed on page xii of the Introduction. In particular, request and read the prospectus, *Pension and Bounty-Land Warrant Files in the National Archives*, publication # 60-9.

At the National Archives the printed *Index of Revolutionary War Pension Applications*, which has been published in the National Genealogical Society Quarterly since March 1943—is available in the Central Search Room. Also, a complete index to the Revolutionary War pensions and bounty land warrants is available on microfilm in the Microfilm Reading Room, second floor, National Archives.

Also, for those individuals who have microfilm readers, or have access to a machine, you may wish to purchase all or parts of the Revolutionary War Index from the Publications and Exhibits Branch, National Archives Records Service, Room G-10, National Archives Building, National Archives, Washington 25, D.C. This branch has available a free book entitled, *List of National Archives Microfilm Publications*, 1961, publication #61-12. The book contains also order forms for microfilm purchases.

For those persons who wish to order a single pension-bounty land record instructions are given on page xiii and xiv of the Introduction. These instructions apply specifically to those persons ordering by correspondence.

The National Society, Daughters of the American Revolution Library at 1776 D Street, N.W. Washington 6, D.C. has an excellent library and facilities for records pertaining to the Revolutionary War. For non-members the daily search fee is $1.00 the library being open Tuesday through Friday of the week.

POST REVOLUTIONARY WAR PERIOD, 1784-1811

(Source: *Preliminary Inventory of the Records of the Adjutant General's Office*, Inventory #17, Washington: 1949.)

Carded Military Service Records, 1784-1903 (page 99) Post-Revolutionary War Period, 1784-1811 Jackets showing name of soldier, organization and rank, and containing cards on which information relating to the individual obtained from muster and pay rolls and other original records has been copied. Arranged alphabetically by States furnishing troops, thereunder by commanding officer's name, and thereunder alphabetically by name of soldier.

"Indexes to the carded records, volunteer organizations, consist of alphabetical name indexes showing name of organization, rank and dates of service. Arranged in the following files: (1) General Index containing names of all individuals having service for the period 1784-1811; (2) indexes to the following separate groups: Organizations from the Territory South of the Ohio, 1793-94; Lieutenant Colonel Harmer's First U.S. Regiment, 1785-90; Lieutenant Colonel Darke's First U.S. Levies, 1791-94; and Colonel Gibson's Second U.S. Levies, 1791-92 and (3) general index to State organizations arranged under individual States or groups of States.

Note: These records are currently available at the Military & Navy Service Branch, second floor, room W-7-1, National Archives and *are not* on microfilm.

USE AND AVAILABILITY OF REVOLUTIONARY WAR RECORDS

Throughout this book will be found reproductions of actual file records from the National Archives. They are reproduced herein so that an individual might see the nature of the records, that they are for the most part in a manuscript form and, more important, the information that they contain. Notice in particular that in any widow's application, or declaration, for bounty land or for pension benefits that she must prove her marriage to the soldier, her husband. To the genealogist note in particular that the *place* of marriage is given and if there is not a sworn statement by the county clerk of the county where the marriage took place then affidavits must accompany the application to certify to the marriage. Under the reproduced copies of records for the section pertaining to the War of 1812, notice the full page of instruction to one Mary Pugh, widow of Daniel Pugh, and what she must do or comply with in order to establish her proof of marriage.

In other of these reproduced documents, especially the later ones, the veteran is required to list the places of residence since his military duty. Also, in the later documents note particularly that the widow will give her maiden name. These are just a few of the salient and valuable parts of these declarations and applications for bounties from military service.

Just as an example, or sample, of the papers that might be found in a file I have taken the following list from the file of the pensioner Frederick Shaver, # S. (soldier) 32,517. All files do not have so many papers but notice here-below the tid-bits of genealogical information that can be found in the complete file. Watch for names, relationships between people, places and dates.

1. Declaration of soldier—24 July 1833—for Act of Congress 7 June 1832.
2. Letter of transmittal of pension application to Clerk of Court to Honorable Lewis Cass, Secretary of War.
3. Certification to pension by Lewis Cass, Secretary of War.

4. Letter written by S. D. Manwell, to Senator A. S. White from Frankfort, Indiana to Washington City.
5. Application for a transfer (a form) signed by soldier—giving present address in Indiana, requesting pension to be transferred there from Tennessee giving reasons for transfer.
6. Letter of transmittal for item #5 by Senator A. W. White to J. L. Edwards, Commissioner of Pensions.
7. Letter (a form) of Treasury Department, 21 June 1843, regarding statement of pensioner.
8. Letter from Knoxville Agency Office to Commissioner of Pensions regarding last payment through that office.
9. (a form) War Department Pension Office to soldier requesting additional proof of service with (printed) instructions as to how this can be done.
10. Original Bounty Land Warrant (cancelled because soldier died before its issuance) for 160 acres as private in Revolutionary War. The following is the text of the original Bounty Land Warrant.

"United States of America, Department of Interior, Office of the Commissioner of Pensions, it is hereby certified that under the Act of March 3, 1855, entitled "an act in addition to certain acts granting Bounty Land to certain officers and soldiers who have been engaged in the military service of the United States—(space for soldier's name) is entitled to locate one hundred and sixty acres, at any Land Office of the United States, in one body, and in conformity to the legal sub-divisions of the public lands, upon any of the public lands subject to sale at either the minimum or lower graduated prices." (At the bottom of the certificate there is a place to enter the location of the land.)

11. Application by soldier for land warrant due with statement by two persons regarding identity of soldier sworn to before Clerk of Circuit Court.

12. Letter of transmittal for Bounty Land applications.
13. Statement regarding spelling of the name "Shaver" saying it is sometimes "Shever" and other times "Shaffer".
14. Letter to Commissioner of Pensions regarding Bounty Lands due heirs of soldier, 15 June 1858.
15. Letter to Senate and House of Representatives of the Congress of the U.S. by B. A. Shaffer, "youngest son" of deceased soldier, petitioning for bounty land. dated 9 August 1856.
16. Letter to Commissioner of Pensions by John Barnet regarding acknowledgment of receipt of Bounty Land Warrant ,1 Sept. 1856.
17. Slip of paper giving number of Bounty Land Warrant #17, 1855 for 160 acres.
18. Small brown envelope regarding papers, date of Act, Bounty Land, etc.
19. Small brown folder (jacket) regarding pension information.
20. Letter of transmittal of request for Bounty Land by Benjamin A. Shaffer to Commissioner of Pensions.
21. Form letter reply giving infromation regarding soldier's service, etc.
22. Carbon copy of letter to descendant, in Frankrort, Indiana, a great granddaughter of soldier, regarding his service, dated 24 June 1936.
23. Carbon copy of letter to descendant in DesMoines, Iowa, by Winfield Scott, Commissioner, dated 28 January 1927.
24. Carbon copy of letter to descendant in Olympia, Washington, regarding death of soldier, dated 25 Feb. 1905, from acting commissioner of pensions.
25. Original letter of descendant from DesMoines, Iowa, to Bureau of Pensions regarding Revolutionary War service of soldier, dated 22 May 1936.

24. Carbon copy of letter to descendant in Olympia, Washington, regarding death of soldier, dated 25 Feb. 1905, from acting commissioner of pensions.

25. Original letter of descendant from DesMoines, Iowa, to Bureau of Pensions regarding Revolutionary War service of soldier, dated 22 May 1936.

26. Original letter of descendant from Frankfort, Indiana, regarding soldier, dated 17 January 1927.

27. Jacket slip from Record and Pension Office to descendant regarding soldier's service, dated 19 Dec. 1899.

28. Original letter from descendant at Olympia, Washington, to Department of Interior requesting information about soldier's service, dated 17 June 1913.

29. Original leter of descendant from Lima, Ohio, to Pension Office regarding soldier's service, dated 27 April 1913.

30. Original letter of descendant, etc. from Olympia, Washington, 6 June 1905.

31. Original letter of descendant regarding soldier, from Olympia, Washington, 2 January 1900.

32. A jacket for Invalid file with number, service memos, etc.

State of Tennessee }
Hardeman County } On this the 21st day of May
A.D. One thousand Eight Hun-
dred and fifty three, personally appeared before me M. B. Ruffin
a justice of the peace of said County and state
(and one of the county Court of said County
and state, which is a court of record,) Cynthia
Estes, a resident of Hardeman County and state
aforesaid aged ninety years, who first being duly sworn according to law, doth, on her
oath make the following declaration in order to
obtain the benefits of the provision made by
the act of congress, passed on the 3d of February 1853, granting pensions to widows of persons
who served during the revolutionary war; that
she is the widow of Thomas Estes, who was a
pensioner of the United States under the act of
the 7th of June 1832 at the rate of Eighty dollars
per annum, that the said Thomas Estes was on
the pension roll of the Nashville Agency Tenn.
and that he was paid at said Agency, that
he was placed on said Roll on the day
of 1833 (to the best of her recollection)
and that she refers to the proof now on file
in the pension office at Washington City, to
show the rank of the said Thomas Estes, the time
when he entered and left the service, the names
and rank of the officers under whom the service
was performed, the place in which he resided
when he left the service.
She further declares that she was married to
the said Thomas Estes on the 1st day of July
1812, that her said husband died on the 10th

CHAPTER III

THE PERIOD OF THE WAR OF 1812

"President Madison declared war on 18 June 1812 shouting: "On to Canada" This was called also our second War of Independence. The War of 1812 ended with the Treaty of Ghent and signed on Christmas Eve 1814. Everything was restored to what it had been before the war. "We have obtained nothing but peace."

A. *Provisions of the various acts for pensions, etc.*

(Source: *Federal Military Pensions in the United States,* by William Henry Glasson, Ph.D. Oxford University Press, N.Y. 1918, Chapter V.)

"... but the enlargement of the military forces of the United States in time of actual warfare caused the broadening and extension of the ordinary pension laws to meet the new conditions in each case and to provide benefits for volunteers and militia.

"Various acts reising troops for the War of 1812 promised to the soldiers enlisting the benefits of the same invalid-pension provisions as had been made for the regular army by the Act of 1802 ... before the Civil War pensions had been granted for life to all surviving War of 1812 widows whose husbands had died as a result of wounds received, or of disability incurred, in service.

"Service pensions on account of the War of 1812 were not granted until 1871 for all sailors and soldiers who had served 60 days and were honorably discharged. Applicants were required to have been loyal during the Civil War and to take an oath to support the Constitution. ... the Act of 1878 abolished the requirement of loyalty during the Civil War.

"The last surviving pensioned soldier of the War of 1812 was Hiram Cronk of Ava, Oneida County, N.Y. He died on May 13, 1905 at the age of 105 years. On June 30, 1916 more than a century after the close of the War of 1812, 115 widows remained on the pension roll.

Among the National Archives Microfilm publications is pamphlet #313 (an explanation) of the *Index to War of 1812 Pension Application Files*. This pamphlet lists the roll numbers (for microfilm) for the alphabet A-Z, rolls #1-102. The following is the Preface to this publication of roll numbers and it is reproduced here as a matter of information in general although it is an explanation of the microfilm index itself.

"Reproduced on the 102 rolls if this microfilm publication are the faces of the envelopes containing War of 1812 pension application files. On the face of each envelope are the name of the veteran, the pension claim or file numbers, and other identifying information. In addition there are cross-reference cards for veterans' names that appear under more than one spelling and for names of substitutes who served for another soldier. Since the envelopes and cards are arranged alphabetically by name of veteran, this microfilm serves as an index to the records.

"The pension application files for the War of 1812 are one of several series of records in the National Archives relating to applications for or benefits granted to veterans who rendered military or naval service, or to their survivors. Following the precetent set for Revolutionary War veterans, Congress authorized pensions for those who served in the War of 1812. Congress also passed laws that authorized the granting of warrants for land to those who have served in the War of 1812 and other early wars.

"The pension application files in the War of 1812 series r 'ate to claims based on service rendered between 1812 and 1815. Most of the applications were filed under the acts of February 14, 1871 (16 Stat. 411) and March 9, 1878 (20 Stat. 27). These were the first acts granted pensions to War of 1812 veterans and their surviving widows on the basi of service alone. Earlier acts had provided benefits only for service-connected death or disability. The Act of 1871 granted pensions to surviving soldiers and sailors who had served 60 days in the War of 1812 and had been honorably discharged, or to those who had been personally named in any resolution by Congress for specific service of less than 60 days. The widows of such soldiers and sailors were eligible for pension provided the marriage had taken place before the treaty of peace was ratified on February 17, 1815. Ahe act of 1878 provided pensions for surviving soldiers and sailors of the War of 1812 who had served for 14 days or in any engagement and had been honorably discharged and for their surviving widows. It made no proviso regarding the date of marriage.

"All pensions granted to veterans of the War of 1812 and their surviving dependents before 1871 were based exclusively on service-connected death or disability. The pension provisions already in existence for veterans of the regular and volunteer forces were applied to veterans of the War of 1812 and to their surviving dependents by acts of January 29, 1812 (2 Stat. 794) and April 16, 1816 (3 Stat. 285) Other similar or supplementary acts providing benefits on account of death or disability were passed by Congress between 1813 and 1871.

"If a veteran applied for a pension based on service in War of 1812, his file generally contains, in addition to his name, such information as his age, place of residence, service data including dates, places of enlistment and discharge, organization and rank. In addition there are reports by the Adjutant General and the 3rd and 4th Auditors of the Treasury verifying the military or naval service of the veteran. Similar information is contained in the widow's application file, which also generally shows the widow's age and maiden name, the date and place of marriage, and the date and place of the veteran's death. The file will contain all pension applications that were based on the service of the same veteran in the War of 1812. For example, if both applied for benefits, it will contain the application of the widow as well as of the veteran. Some of the bounty-land warrant applications files, which contain similar information, have been consolidated with the pension files.

"The amount of information shown on the envelope are the name of the veteran, the name of the widow if she applied, the pension claim or file number or numbers, and some indication either of the type of service or of the organization in which the veteran served. Many of the envelopes also give certain personal identifying data about the veteran and/or his widow. Information given in the upper right-hand corner of some envelopes relates to applications for bounty land. A file, however, may contain bounty-land applications even though there is no such indication on the envelope.

" The pension and bounty-land warrant application files, the envelopes of which are reproduced in this microcopy, are part of a body of records in the National Archives designated as Record Group 15, Records of the Veterans' Administration. In the same group there is a series of bounty-land warrant application files that include a considerable number of applications based on War of 1812 service that *were not* consolidated with the pension applications. There is also a series of "Old Wars" application files relating to claims based on death or disability incurred in service in the early wars. In this series are a few files of Regular Army soldiers whose service included the War of 1812, but began before 1812 or continued after 1815.

"There are related files in other record groups in the National Archives. In record group 94, Records of the Office of the Adjutant General, are compiled service records of volunteer soldiers and also records relating to soldiers who served in the Regular Army. Records relating to naval and marine service during the War of 1812 and included in Record Group 45, Naval Records Collection of the Office of Naval Records and Library, and Record Group 127, Records of the United States Marine Corps. The original warrants issued to veterans under the military bounty-land warrant acts are in Record Group 49, Records of the Bureau of Land Management."

PERIOD OF THE WAR OF 1812

B—*Bounties for service, etc.*

Note: this subject for the War of 1812 is treated in the Introduction on page xx in some detail.

C—*Use and availability of the records.*

For those persons who correspond with the National Archives for military information it is suggested that you follow the instructions on pages xiii and xiv of the Introduction. Otherwise searchers must go to the Central Search Room of the National Archives, secure a searcher's pass, and thereafter use the microfilm index for this war as explained on the last few pages.

Also, there are a number of published lists for veterans of wars as found in the larger libraries. Once you have secured the identifying information from these published lists you may thereafter inquire for the records that were made as a result of his military or naval service.

It should also be mentioned here of the availability of the following records as found in the National Archives as identified in the *Preliminary Inventory of the Records of the Adjutant General's Office*, #17, 1949, page 100,

"Carded Records, Volunteer Organizations; War of 1812 . . . jackets showing name of soldier, organization and rank, and containing cards on which information relating to the individual obtained from muster rolls, pay rolls, and various other original records has been copied. Personal papers, if any, are filed in smaller jackets and included in the main jackets.

"Indexes to the carded records, volunteer organizations: War of 1812, giving name of soldier, organization, and rank, together with cross-reference information. Arranged in two files: (1) General alphabetical index and (2) an alphabetical index for each State, U.S. Volunteers, Indians, Prisoners of War, Quartermaster Department and Spies. The first index includes all the names appearing in the second.

Note: Only the index to the above is available in the Microfilm Reading Room, National Archives. The records are available through the Military and Navy Service Branch (Military Service Records), Room 7-W, National Archives.

*   *   *

On the four pages that follow are reproduced original records from the files of the War of 1812. Notice that the first two are for the veteran and his widow. Note that the marriage information is in the widow's application. Note also that the #3 document for Mary Pugh has required an additional statement for proof of marriage and that the document #4 shows the manner in which this might be secured by the applicant. The form also indicates other records that might be found in other files in order to meet this requirement. These documents are not complete but rather the most part of the first page of the application.

Declaration for Pension.

1.

STATE OF NEW YORK,
County of Tompkins, } ss.

On this *28d* day of *March*, A. D., one thousand eight hundred and seventy *one*, personally appeared before me *Clerk of the Supreme Court* of the *said County*, a court of record within and for the county and State aforesaid, *Nathan Smith*, aged *81* years, a resident of *Newfield*, county of *Tompkins*, State of *New York*, who, being duly sworn according to law, declares that he is married, that his wife's name was *Hulda Newman*, to whom he was married at *Pawlings*, on the *14th* day of *Jany.* 181*5*; that he served the full period of sixty days in the *militia* service of the United States in the war of 1812; that he is the identical *Nathan Smith* who *was drafted a private* in Captain *John Platts* company, *Col. Anthony Delmater* regiment, *New York Militia* brigade, division, at *Poughkeepsie* on the day of *Aug.* 181*4*, and was honorably discharged at *New York* on the day of *November*, 1814; that *he served at Harlem Heights.*

Applied for and recd. land warrant under act 1850 of 40 acers No. 5,692 also under act of 1855 land warrant for 120 acers No. 2,561

that he, at no time during the late rebellion against the authority of the United States, adhered to the cause of the enemies of the Government, giving them aid or comfort; or exercised the functions of any office whatever under any authority, or pretended authority, in hostility to the United

(WAR OF 1812.)

Declaration of a Widow for Pension.

————

2.

State of *Pennsylvania*,   }
County of *Bradford*,   } ss.

War of 1812 – Declaration of widow of soldier, previous page. Note: Wife's maiden name date and place of marriage, etc. death–place & date for husband

On this **24th** day of *January*, A. D., one thousand eight hundred and seventy- *two*, personally appeared before me, *an Associate Judge, of Common Plea*, of the *said county*, a court of record in and for the county and State aforesaid, *Huldah Smith*, aged **83** years, a resident of *Newfield*, county of *Tompkins*, State of *New York*, who, being duly sworn according to law, declares that she is the widow of *Nathan Smith* who served the full period of sixty days in the *New York Militia* service of the United States in the war of 1812, and who was the identical *Nathan Smith* who *was a Private* in Captain *John Platts* company, Col *Anthony Delamater* regiment, *New York Militia mustered at Pokepsen* Married. at *Haerlem N.Y.*, on the day of *August* 1814; that *he served and discharged in Nov 1814 and make Claim for a Pension No 3416 under act of Feby 14 1871 and received Pension Certificate payable at Canandaigua N.Y.* that she was married under the name of *Huldah Newman* to said *Nathan Smith*, on the *fourteenth* day of *January* A. D., 18**15**, by *one Bushnell a Minister of the Gospel* at *Pawlings N.Y.*, there being no legal barrier to such marriage; that her said husband died at *Newfield*, on the **10** day of *September*, 187**1**, and that she has not remarried since his death, : that at no time during the late rebellion against the authority of the United States did she

WAR OF 1812.

Claim of Widow for Pension, under the Provisions of Sections 4736 to 4740 inclusive Revised Statutes, and the Act of March 9, 1878.

3.

State of _West Virginia_ }
County of _Hancock_ } ss.

On this _22nd_ day of _March_, A. D. one thousand eight hundred and _Seventy Eight_ personally appeared before me, _Clerk of the Circuit Court_, the same being a **Court of Record** within and for the county and State aforesaid, (1) _Mary Pugh_ aged _85_ years, a resident of _Hancock County_, in the State of _West Virginia,_ who, being duly sworn according to law, declares that she is a widow of (2) _Captain Davis Pugh_ deceased, who was the identical (3) _Capt Davis Pugh_, who served under the name of (4) _Capt. Davis Pugh_ as a (5) _Captain_ in the company commanded by Captain _Davis Pugh_, in the regiment of _Virginia Militia_ commanded by _____ in the war of 1812; that her said husband (6) _Volunteered_ at _Brooke Co. Va_ on or about the _____ day of _____, A. D. _____, for the term of _____, and continued in actual service in said war for the term of (7) _____, and whose services terminated, by reason of (8) _____ at _____, on the _____ day of _____, A. D. _____. She further states that the following is a full description of her said husband at the time of his enlistment, viz: (9) _No Description to be found_

_____. She further states that she was married to the said _Davis Pugh_, at the city (or town) of _Fairview_, in the county of _Hancock_ and in the State of _West Virginia_, on the _21st_ day of _March_ A. D. _1815_, by one (10) _Rev. George Scott_, who was a (11) _Presbyterian Minister_ and that her name before her said marriage was _Mary Snowden_; and she further states that (12) _her said husband was never Married but the One Time_ and that her said husband (13) _Davis Pugh_, died at _Hancock Co._, in the State of _West Virginia_, on the _20th_ day of _April_, A. D. _1855_; and she further declares that the following have been the places of residence of herself and her said husband since the date of his discharge from the Army, viz: (14) _at Hancock County West Virginia near the Town of Fairview_

She makes this declaration for the purpose of obtaining the pension to which she may be entitled under the provisions of Sections 4736 to 4740 inclusive Revised Statutes, and the Act of March 9, 1878, and hereby constitutes and appoints with full powers of substitution and revocation **T. E. & B. F. LLOYD**, of Washington D. C.

(M.)

Navy, Old War, and Bounty } Land Division. }

{ Service Pension, War of 1812; or Bounty Land Claim.

4.

Department of the Interior,

PENSION OFFICE,

Washington, D. C., _____ *June 7th,* 1878.

Sir:

In the claim of *Mary Pugh, widow of David*
for a _____ *Pension* _____ under act of *March 9, 1878, No. 961* _____
proof of *her* marriage to the soldier is required. You are informed that proof upon
this point is of value in the following order:

1. A certified copy of a church or other public record.

2. An affidavit of the officiating clergyman or magistrate.

3. A copy of family record, sworn to by custodian, certified by the magistrate
to be correct, and that the original appears to be genuine. When this class of evidence is furnished it must be shown by whom and when the record was made, and
the date of the Bible, or other book, in which the record is made, must be given.

4. The testimony of two or more eye-witnesses of the ceremony.

5. Affidavits of children whose ages would show the date of marriage or
commencement of cohabitation.

6. The testimony of two or more witnesses who know the parties to have lived
together as husband and wife from the date of their alleged marriage, the witnesses
stating the period during which they knew them thus to cohabit.

Witnesses under the 4th, 5th, and 6th classes of testimony must state the circumstances or cotemporaneous events by which they are enabled to fix the date of the
marriage.

Before any of the lower classes of evidence can be accepted, it must be shown
by competent testimony that none higher can be obtained.

In all affidavits relative to marriage, the affiants should state their ages at the
time they testify.

If the claim is for service pension under the act of February 14, 1871,
marriage must be proved at a date prior to February 17, 1815.

If the claim is for service pension under either the act of February 14, 1871,
or March 9, 1878, continuous widowhood since the death of the soldier for whose
service the claim is made must be proved.

If the claim is for Bounty Land, widowhood at the time of making the application must be proved.

Return this Circular with the evidence.

Very respectfully,

J. A. Bentley

Commissioner.

Ths. E. Lloyd, Esq.

CHAPTER IV

THE PERIOD OF THE INDIAN WARS

A. *Provisions of the acts, etc.*

Source: *Federal Military Pensions in the United States,* by William Henry Glasson, Ph.D. Oxford University Press, N.Y. 1918, page 114, as follows:

"Many of these armed conflicts with hostile Indian tribes have been of sufficient importance to be termed wars. It has been the custom of Congress to extend the benefits of exicting pension laws to soldiers disabled on such campaigns and also to the widows and orphans of the slain.

". . . an early example of such provisions for those engaged in fighting hostile Indians was the Act of 1812 for the relief of officers and soldiers who served in General Harrisons campaign on the Wabash, the victors of the Battle of Tippacanoe. From that time down to the Civil War the benefits of the invalid-pension laws were frequently extended to those engaged in putting down Indian insurrections in Florida, Illinois, Wisconsin and other States.

"Service-pensions were not granted on account of the Indian Wars until the passage of the Act of July 27, 1892. This measure was for the benefit of those "who served for 30 days in the Black Hawk War, the Creek War, the Cherokee disturbances or the Florida War with the Seminole Indians between 1832-1843 and were honorably discharged.

"An Act of June 27, 1902 extended the benefits of the above law to the surviving officers and enlisted men who served thirty days or more under the U.S. Military,

State, Territorial or Provincial authorities in a considerable number of Indian Wars fought between 1817 and 1858.

✳

B—*Bounties for military service, etc.*

Note: this subject is treated at length in the Introduction, page xix.

THE PERIOD OF THE INDIAN WARS

C—*The Use and Availability of the Records.*

By correspondence these records are available through the instructions as given in the Introduction pages xiii and xiv and the use of the form NA-288. Otherwise, the indexes are available through the Microfilm Reading Room, Central Reading Room, second floor, National Archives.

However, from the publication, *Preliminary Inventory of the Records of the Adjutant General's Office,* #17, Washington, 1949, the following carded records are available through the Military and Navy Service Branch (Military Service Records) Room W-7, second floor, National Archives Building. The records described as follows *are not* on microfilm and constitute a military-service type of record and not a pension-type of record.

Page 101 "Indian Wars, 1817-1858, Carded Records, Volunteer Organizations, . . . jackets showing name of soldier, organization, and rank and containing cards on which information from returns, muster rolls, pay rolls, and other records was copied relating to the military service of the individual . . . Very few personal papers are to be found in this file. Arranged by State, thereunder by wars, (including Florida Wars, Black Hawk War, and others), thereunder by organization and thereunder alphabetically by name of the soldier.

"... included in this file and similarly arranged are the carded records for a few organizations such as the Battalion of the United States Volunteers, engaged in the "Utah Expedition, 1857-58," and the New York and Michigan Volunteer organizations that did boundary duty during the Canadian "Patriotic War", 1838-39.

"... Index to (above) records (Indian Wars, 1817-58) ... give name of soldier, name of war in which individual had service, organization, and rank. Arranged alphabetically in two files; (1) General Index containing all the names of persons serving in the various Indian Wars and (2) indexes arranged under each State that furnished troops separately for each war. The general index contains all the names appearing in the State indexes . . . including the Utah Expedition and the Patriot War.

✳

Examples of Records on the following pages:

To acquaint the researcher with the general nature of the files for this war, examples of the *first page only* of three files are given. Note that pages, or examples, #2 and #3 are for the husband (in his lifetime) and the widow's application after his death. Note also that Richard Presley states where he has lived since leaving the service. Here it states State only but commonly it names city and county of former residence.

Example #1 is of particular interest to the author inasmuch as it is the first page of the Indian War application of his grandfather. Later this application was "rejected" because he could not prove that he was in this war. The applicant explains to the Commissioner of Pensions that, at the time, the soldiers in the local militia were more interested in defending their homes and families than they were in being placed on the muster roll of the militia. He told me many true-life stories from this war and his part in it.

DECLARATION FOR SURVIVOR'S PENSION—INDIAN WARS.

Acts of July 27, 1892, June 27, 1902, May 30, 1908, and March 4, 1917.

State of _Utah_, County of _Utah_,

On this _7_ day of _July_, 1917, personally appeared before me, a _Notary Public_ within and for the County and State aforesaid, _James Kirkham_, who, being duly sworn by me according to law, declares that he is _68_ years of age; that he was born _August 28th 1849_, 1 _London England_; and that he is _____ an actual and bona fide resident _Lehi Utah_, County, State of _Utah_

That he is the identical person who enlisted at _Lehi Utah_ under the name of _James Kirkham_, on the _3d_ day of _March_, 1866 as a _Privt_ (Rank.) in _Cavalry under the command of Washburn Chipman of American Fork Utah_ (Here describe fully the organization in which service was rendered.) and was honorably discharged _march 22d_, 1866, at _Lehi Utah_, having served thirty days or more in the war or disturbance with, or campaign against, the _Black Hawk_ Indians, in the State (or Territory) of _Utah_

That he also served _as a home guard from April 1st 1865 to nov 1 1866_ (Here give a complete statement of all other military or naval service, if any, at whatever time rendered.) _I was again Enlisted to Serve a number of Days by an Order from Leut Gen D.H. Well Dated June 6 1866 Salt Lake City Ut I went on the trip_

That otherwise than as herein stated he was _____ employed in the United States service.

That his personal description at time of first enlistment was as follows: Height, _5_ feet, _9_ inches; complexion, _light_; color of eyes, _blue_; color of hair, _light_; that his occupation was _Farmer_. That since leaving the service he has resided at _Lehi City Utah County Utah also for about 4 years in Canada from 1900 to 1904 Since then in Utah_ his occupation has been _Postmaster and Merchandising_

That he has _____ applied for pension under Original No. _____ That he is _____ a pensioner under Certificate No. _____

That he makes this declaration for the purpose of being placed on the pension roll of the United States under the provisions of the ACTS OF CONGRESS GRANTING PENSION TO SURVIVORS OF CERTAIN WARS AND DISTURBANCES WITH AND CAMPAIGNS AGAINST INDIANS FROM 1817 TO JANUARY, 1891, INCLUSIVE.

(Two attesting and identifying witnesses.)

(1) _Elisha H Davis_ (Signature of first witness.) _Lehi Utah Co Utah_ (Address of first witness.)

(2) _A. F. Crawford_ (Signature of second witness.) _Lehi, Utah Co, Utah_ (Address of second witness.)

James Kirkham (Claimant's signature in full.)

Lehi City Utah Co Utah (Claimant's address in full.)

INDIAN WARS.

2.

Claim of Soldier for Service Pension Under Act of July 27, 1892.

To be executed before some officer authorized to administer oaths for general purposes. The official character and signature of any such officer not required by law to use a seal must be certified by the clerk of the proper court, giving dates of beginning and close of official term.

A full and explicit reply is required to all questions indicated by this blank.

STATE OF _Arkansas_

County of _Boone_ } ss.

On this _13_ day of _May_, A. D. one thousand eight hundred and ninety-_____,

personally appeared before me, a _Notary Public_ in and for the County and State aforesaid,

Richard Presley, aged _74_ years, a resident of _Batavia_,

in the State of _Arkansas_, who, being duly sworn according to law, declares that he is the

identical person who served under the name of _Richard Presley_, as a _Privat_

in the company commanded by Capt. _J. B. Chasteen_, in the _first_ Regiment of

Georgia vol, commanded by _Eligu Chasteen_, in the

If in the Navy, name vessels.

Florida War; that he enlisted at _Blairsvill union co_, on or about the

last day of _September_, A. D. 18_37_, for the term of _Six Months_,

_____, and was honorably discharged at _Camp Call, Hall co Ga_ on the

_15H_ day of _March_, A. D. 18_38_; that he also served in _____ Co.,

_____ Regt., _____ Vols., from _____,

18____; to _____, 18____; and in _____ Co., _____

Regt., _____ Vols., from _____, 18____; to _____

_____, 18____; that he has not been employed in the military or naval service of the United States other-

wise than as stated above.

That at the time of entering the service claimed for he was _19_ years of age, _Six_ feet _____

inches in height, with _blue_ eyes, _Sandy_ hair, _light_ complexion, by occupation a

Farmer, and that he was born at _____, County of

Buncombe, State of _North Carolina_

That since leaving the service he has resided _in the State of Tennesse_, _5_ years,

and in Georgia, _30_ years, _in Arkensaw_ _22_

years, at _____, _____ years, and at _____

That he was married to _Mary Grizzel_ on the _20th_ day of

December, A. D. 18_38_, _in Lumphins co Ga_; that his said wife is

now _living_, having died on the _____ day of _____,

INDIAN WARS. *3.*

Claim of Widow for Service Pension Under Act of July 27, 1892.

To be executed before some officer authorized to administer oaths for general purposes. The official character and signature of any such officer not required by law to use a seal must be certified by the clerk of the proper court, giving dates of beginning and close of official term.
A full and explicit reply is required to all questions indicated by this blank.

State of *Arkansas*, County of *Bone*, ss:

On this *5th* day of *August*, A. D. 189*5*, personally appeared before me, a *Notary Public* within and for the county and State aforesaid, *Marcy. M. Presley* aged *72* years, a resident of *Batavia Bone Co*, in the State of *Arkansas*, who, being duly sworn according to law, declares that she is the widow of *Richard Presley* deceased, who was the identical person who served under the name of *Richard Presley* as a *Privat* in the company commanded by Capt. *Chastains Co Ga. Vols* in the _____ Regiment of _____, commanded by *Capt. Chastine*, (If in the Navy, name vessels.) in the *Indian* war; that her said husband enlisted at *Delonaga. Lumphins co Ga* _____ day of _____, A. D. 18*37*, for the term of _____, and was discharged at _____ on the _____ day of _____ A. D. 18_____; that he also served in Capt. *Chastins* Co., Regt., _____ Vols.; from _____, 18_____, to _____, 18_____, and in Capt. _____ Co., _____ Regt., Vols., from _____, 18_____, to _____, 18_____; that he was not otherwise employed in the military or naval service of the United States.

That at the time of entering the service claimed for, her said husband was *19* years of age, _____ feet _____ inches in height, with _____ eyes, _____ hair, _____ complexion, by occupation a *Farmer*, and that he was born *on French braad River* county of *Bunsom*, State of *North Carolina*

That after leaving the service he resided *in Lundins co Ga, 34* years, at _____ years, at _____ years, and *came to ark some time in 1871*

That she was married to him on the *20th* day of *December*, A. D. 18*38*, at *Delonaga Lumphins Co Ga,* under the name of *Marcy. M. Guggld*; that he had *not* been previously married *and that She never was Divorced*; that she had *not* been previously married; *and she has not remarried since his death*

That her said husband died at *Batavia ark* on the *18th* day of *June*, A. D. 189*5*; that she has *not* since remarried—to wit, to _____ on the _____ day of _____, A. D. 18_____.

That she has *not* heretofore made application for pension; that the number of her claim is _____; that she has *not* made application for bounty land, the number of her land warrant being _____; that her husband *did has pensioner, and the number of his certificate was* make application for pension, the number of his claim being *30110*

CHAPTER V

THE PERIOD OF THE MEXICAN WAR

Mexican War: 26 April 1846 to 2 February 1848. The annexation of Texas was equivalent to a declaration of war against the Mexican Republic. In the treaty that was signed, not only did our government gain the disputed area on the Rio Grande and Nuecos Rivers, but also the vast Mexican Cession which included the present day California, New Mexico, Arizona, Nevada, Utah and parts of Colorado and Wyoming. In return Mexico was paid $15,000,000 and some $3,000,000 of her debts were assumed by the United States.

A—*Provisions of the acts, etc.*

(Source: *Federal Military Pensions in the United States,* by William Henry Glasson, Ph.D. Oxford University Press, N.Y. 1918.

"When the war broke out in 1846 between Mexico and the United States, an Act of May 13, 1846 authorized the President to raise volunteers for the prosecution of the war. A section of this act promised to the volunteers, who should be wounded, or otherwise disabled in the services, benefit of the same pension provisions as were in force for regular troops. . . . in 1858 the half-pay of widows was extended for life and of orphans until they reached the age of 16 years. At the time of the Civil War invalid pensions were granted for service in the Mexican War on the same basis as for service in the War of 1812 and Indian Wars.

". . . the advocates of service-pensions on account of the Mexican War finally achieved success in the passage of the Act of January 29, 1887. This law applied to persons who being duly enlisted actually served 60 days with the army or navy of the United States in Mexico, or on the coasts or frontiers thereof, or in route thereto, in the war with that nation, or were actually engaged in said war and were honorably discharged, and to such other officers and soldiers or sailors as may have been personally named in any resolution of Congress for any specific service in said war, and the surviving widows of such officers and enlisted men.

"Survivors of the War with Mexico were granted age and service pensions by the Act of Feb. 6, 1907. The length of service required was 60 days with an honorable discharge."

B—*Bounties for service, etc.*

Note: See Introduction, pages xix and following for this information.

C—*The Use and Availability of the records.*

By correspondence the records are available through the instructions given on pages xiii and xiv of this book and the subsequent use of the form NA-288.

At the National Archives the records are available in the Microfilm Reading Room, Second Floor. The Record Group #15 is for the *pensions* of this war that were filed between the years 1887 to 1926. These two statements pertain to the indexes only. After the proper file numbers have been secured, the records are available through the Reference Desk, Central Search Room.

The above index to Mexican War pensions includes also the pensions for the so-called "Mormon Battalion". The service records of this battalion are available on microfilm but the pension files have not been microfilmed. However, *an index* to the *service* and *pension* records of this battalion will be published by Mrs. June B. (Florian) Thayn of 2708 Cheverly Avenue, Cheverly, Maryland. The index is expected to be ready for purchase about March 1965.

From the publication *Preliminary Inventory of the Records of the Adjutant General's Office*, #17, Washington, 1949, page 102 the following is extracted:

"Carded records, volunteer organization, Mexican War . . . jackets giving name of soldier, organization, and rank and containing cards on which information relating to the individual's military service, taken from original records such as return and muster rolls, has been copied. The jackets contain very few personal papers in contrast to the carded records for the Civil War.

". . . index to the carded records, volunteer organization, Mexican War. Card showing name of soldier, organization and rank. Arranged in one alphabet by name of soldier.

Note: at present only the Mormon Battalion portion of these carded service records are available on microfilm. Otherwise the records are available through the Military and Navy Service Branch (Military Service Records) Room W-7, second floor, National Archives.

Examples of records to follow:

On the following page is reproduced the first page of the widow's pension application for the Mexican War. Note the places of birth for the foreign born persons, dates, ministers names, etc.

Act of January 29, 1887.

DECLARATION FOR WIDOW'S PENSION.

STATE OF...... Illinois ....
COUNTY OF...... St. Clair ....} ss:

On this...... 8th ....day of......December.........., A. D. one thousand nine hundred and.. Seventeen personally appeared before me, a......... Notary Public ....within and for the county and State aforesaid, ... Barbara Riess ...., aged.. 88 years, a resident of...... Mascoutah Township ......, county of...... St. Clair ......, State of......... Illinois ...., who, being duly sworn according to law, makes the following declaration in order to obtain pension under the provisions of the ACT OF CONGRESS APPROVED JANUARY 29, 1887.

That she is the widow of............ Adam Riess ...., who was ...... enrolled ....(Enrolled or commissioned)...under the name of............ Adam Riess ...., at Jefferson City, Missouri ....., on the.................day of............................, 1846, as a...... Private ....in...Co. "C" Battalion, Missouri Volunteer Inf. ...., and honorably discharged...................................., 18.46 having rendered such service during the Mexican War. XXXXXXXXXXX ....That the papers filed in my former claim under No. W.O. 20,494 which was rejected on the ground that service was not rendered during Civil War, and which papers are by reference made a part hereof.

That he was not in the military or naval service of the United States otherwise than as stated above.

That he was born on the. 7th .day of.. April ......, 18 29, at.. Altheim, Germany That she was married under the name of......... Barbara Friess .... to said soldier at.. Mascoutah, Illinois ......, on the.......... 31st ....day of...... May ...., 18 53 by...... Rev. Sigmund Spies ....; that there was no legal barrier to the marriage; that she had... not .been previously married; that the soldier had... not .... been previously married, ...(If there was a prior marriage of either, the date and place of death or divorce of former consort or consorts should be stated.)

and that neither she nor said soldier married otherwise than as stated above.

That the said soldier died.. September 24, 1917.. Mascoutah Township, St. Clair Co., Ill that she was not divorced from him, and that she has not remarried since his death.

That she has been disabled since 18 , by reason of...... rheumatism, deafness, and trouble of right eye.

That she has................been dependent upon her labor for support.

That her income from all sources except her own labor is $.. 260.00 .... per year.

That her husband was a pensioner under Certificate No.. 2962

That he did. not .make application for bounty land, the number of his warrant being,. to her best knowledge.

That she has........heretofore applied for pension.. based upon the same service as this application, but under the law of April 19, 1908 as amended by Act of Sept. 8, 1916 and the number thereof being Wid. Orig. 20,494 which was rejected That her post-office address is........... Mascoutah, R.R.#1 ......, County of.... St. Clair .... State of.... Illinois ....

Attest: (1)...   _Barbara Riess_
                                                                (Claimant's signature in full.)
(2)...

Also personally appeared............ Elizabeth Kissel ...., residing in Mascoutah, Illinois ...., and........ Marie Hoering ...., residing in Mascoutah, Illinois ...., persons whom I certify to be respectable and entitled to credit, and who, being by me duly sworn, say they were present and saw............ Barbara Riess ...., the claimant, sign her name (or XXXXXXXX) to the foregoing declaration; that they have every reason to believe, from the appearance of said claimant and their acquaintance with her of.. 66 .....years and.. 70 .... years, respectively, that she is the identical person she represents herself to be, and that they have no interest in the prosecution of this claim.

Attest: Edgar C. Grossmann,   Elizabeth X Kissel
                                                    her
        Elmer O. Riess   mark
                                                (Signatures of witnesses.)

CHAPTER VI

THE PERIOD OF THE CIVIL WAR

"Civil War (War of the Rebellion) started 12 April 1861 at Charleston Harbor, Fort Sumter, Virginia. On 9 April 1865 the Confederate Commander Lee surrendered to General Grant. Union States: Main, Vermont, New Hampshire, Massachusetts, Connecticut, Rhode Island, New Jersey, New York, Pennsylvania, Ohio, Indiana, Michigan, Illinois, Iowa, Wisconsin, Minnesota, Oregon, California, Kansas. Confederate States: Virginia, North Carolina, South Carolina, Georgia, Florida, Tennessee, Alabama, Mississippi, Arkansas, Louisiana, Texas. Border States not seceding: Deleware, Maryland, Missouri, Kentucky. Western Virginia separated from Virginia in 1861 and was admitted to the Union as a State in 1863."

A—*Provisions of the Pension Acts.* (Union or federal forces)

Source: *Federal Military Pensions in the United States,* by William Henry Glasson, Ph.D. Oxford Press, N.Y. 1918.

Page 125: "In passing the Act of 1862, Congress founded what has been called in the Bureau Pensions the "General Law pension system". This was the only system of pension laws in force applying to the Civil War until 1890.

"It provides pensions for soldiers who had incurred permanent bodily injury or disability in military service after March 4, 1861. The claimant must show that his disability was incurred as a direct consequence of the performance of his military duty. This system also provides for the widow, children and other dependent relatives of soldiers who died in actual military service, or, after the close of hostilities, from causes which can be directly traced to injuries reecived or disease contacted while in military service.

". . . another system of pensions was inaugurated in 1890 for the benefit of the veterans of Civil War and their dependent relatives.

". . . in many ways the pension law of 1862 was epoch making. Mothers and orphan sisters had never before been provided for in our national legislation.

"The Act of July 14, 1862 provided . . . if a deceased soldier left neither widow nor child, certain other dependent relatives were eligible in succession to receive the pension of $8.00 per month. The order of precedence was . . . first mothers; second fathers; third orphan brothers or sisters under 16 years of age who were to be pensioned jointly if there were more than one.

". . . a widow who had lost her pension by reason of remarriage may even be restored to the pension roll when she again becomes a widow."

*   *   *

Note: as strange as it may seem, surviving dependents of *Confederate* soldiers did receive benefits of our national government. See Act of Congress, June 17, 1957, Voy. I Stat. 107; Act of Congress, May 23, 1958, Vol. 72, Stat. 133.

B—*Bounties from Civil War Service.*

Note: Bounty land was not given for military service "Laws passed by Congress between 1796 and 1855 also authorized the granting of warrants of land to those who had served in the Revolutionary War, the War of 1812, Indian Wars, and the War with Mexico and also for services . . . until March 22, 1852.

C—*The use and availability of the records.*

By correspondence, the pension and military service records of the Civil War are available for the Union forces through the National Archives and Records Services (GSA) National Archives, Washington 25, D.C. As stated on pages xiii and xiv of the Introduction, pamphlets are available that give correct instructions and procedures for ordering copies of the records.

At the National Archives Building, Washington D.C. the General Index to Union pension records is contained in Record Group #15, Microfilm Reading Room. This same index contains also the pension references for the Spanish-American War, the Philippine Insurrection and other qualifying wars of the period.

From the book, *Preliminary Inventory of the Records of the Adjutant General's Office*, #17, Washington, 1949, page 102 we quote as follows:

"Carded records, volunteer organizations, Civil War . . . (have) jackets containing cards on which information relating to the individuals, companies, and regiments of the Volunteer Service of the United States during the Civil War has been copied from original records such as muster rolls, returns, descriptive books, and morning reports. Personal papers consisting chiefly of enlistment papers, substitute certificates, casualty sheets, death reports, prisoner of war papers and miscellaneous correspondence relating to the individual are filed either in the jacket with the carded records relating to the individual . . . or alphabetically by soldier's name.

"General Index, volunteer organizations, Civil War. Index cards, giving name of soldier, organization and rank, together with cross-reference information if the individual belonged to more than one organization during his military service. The great portion of this index is arranged alphabetically by State, thereunder alphabetically by soldier's name. . . . "

Note: there is also an index to Staff Officers, Civil War, arranged alphabetically by name of officer. Also, these two indexes are not now available in microfilm but are in the process of being microfilmed.

As to the availability of lists of soldiers of both the Union and Confederate forces a great many partial lists by county, city, state, etc. have been published and are available through general libraries.

✳

In the Introduction on pages xiii and xiv are listed several publications available pertaining to the services of the National Archives. In particular they have issued a pamphlet #60-10, *Records in the National Archives Relating to Confederate Soldiers*. This pamphlet explains in detail the history of the accessioning of the records to the National Archives, their genealogical value and availability through correspondence and in person at the Archives.

Note also, in the appendix of this book there are several pages given to the availability of Confederate records through State agencies.

Also, keep in mind when reading the instructions pertaining to Confederate records that *military service* records, and in particular for the Confederacy, contain little or no genealogical information.

The National Archives and Records Service, (GSA) has issued a pamphlet accompanying a printed index to these Confederate *Service* records, entitled Microcopy #253, *Consolidated Index to Compiled Service Records of Confederate Soldiers*. This General Index has 535 rolls on microfilm available for direct searching, Microfilm Reading Room, National Archives. For a more detailed explanation of the contents of this index you may wish to request, without cost, a copy of this pamphlet.

C—*Examples of records*

For the Union veteran, on the following three pages are reported but three pages of information from the pension file. As stated previously, many of these files are filled with genealogical information and contribute generously to the family genealogy and history. Many files were disputed by the Commissioner of Pensions and required affidavits for proof of all kinds. Herewith is reproduced a copy of a Family Bible record. The three files, soldier, widow and the Bible record give some idea of what might be found in a Union Veteran file.

ACT OF MAY 11, 1912.
DECLARATION FOR PENSION.

THE PENSION CERTIFICATE SHOULD NOT BE FORWARDED WITH THE APPLICATION.

State of .... New York ....

County of .... Oswego ....

On this 20*th* day of *May*, A. D. one thousand nine hundred and *twelve*, personally appeared before me, a NOTARY PUBLIC .... within and for the county and State aforesaid, *Charles W. Murdock*, who, being duly sworn according to law, declares that he is *75* years of age, and a resident of *Oswego* county of ...., State of *New York*; and that he is the identical person who was ENROLLED at *Oswego* .... under the name of *Charles W. Murdock*, on the *13th* day of *September*, 18*61*, as a *Musician*, in *the 24th Regiment New York Infantry Volunteers*

(Here state rank, and company and regiment in the Army; or vessels, if in the Navy.)

in the service of the United States, in the *Civil* .... war, and was HONORABLY DISCHARGED

(State name of war, Civil or Mexican.)

at *Culpepper*, on the *16th* day of *August*, 186*2*. That he also served *as a Musician in the Band of the 2nd Brigade, 1st Division, 6th Army Corps, Army of the Potomac from the 1st day of Sept 1863 to the 23d day of June, 1865—*

(Here give a complete statement of all other services, if any.)

That he was not employed in the military or naval service of the United States otherwise than as stated above. That his personal description at enlistment was as follows: Height *5* feet *11* inches; complexion, *light*; color of eyes, *blue*; color of hair, *sandy*; that his occupation was *musician*; that he was born *July 15th*, 18*36*, at *Granby, Oswego Co., New York*

That his several places of residence since leaving the service have been as follows: *Oswego and vicinity —*

(State date of each change as nearly as possible.)

That he is a pensioner under certificate No. *565 780*.

That he has .... applied for pension under original No. .... :

That he makes this declaration for the purpose of being placed on the pension roll of the United States under the provisions of the act of May 11, 1912.

That his post-office address is *347 E. Mohawk St. Oswego* county of *Oswego* State of .... New York ....

Charles W. Murdock

(Claimant's signature in full.)

Attest : (1) ....

(2) ....

No. 144

ACT OF APRIL 19, 1908.

DECLARATION FOR WIDOW'S PENSION.

To be executed before a Court of Record or some officer thereof having custody of its seal, a Notary Public, or Justice of the Peace, whose official signature shall be verified by his official seal, and in case he has none, his signature and official character shall be certified by a Clerk of a Court of Record, or a City or County Clerk.

State of _New York_, County of _Oswego_, ss:

On this _20th_ day of _August_ A. D. one thousand nine hundred and _Twelve_, personally appeared before me, a NOTARY PUBLIC, within and for the County and State aforesaid, _E. Jennie Murdoch_ aged _73_ years, a
(Insert name of applicant.)
resident of _Oswego_ County of _Oswego_ State of
(Name of town or city.)
New York who, being duly sworn according to law, declares that she is the widow of
Charles W. Murdoch who enlisted under the name of _Charles_
(Name of Soldier)
W. Murdoch, on the _13th_ day of _September_ A. D.
(Name under which soldier enlisted.)
18 _61_, as a _Musician_ in Company _the Band_ in the _24th_ Regiment of
(Here state rank.)   (Letter of Company.)   (No. of Regiment.)
New York Regt, Infy Vols and served at least ninety days in the late War
(Name of State, and whether Infantry, Cavalry, Artillery or name of vessel if in Navy.)
of the Rebellion, in the service of the United States, who was HONORABLY DISCHARGED _August 16th_
(Date of Discharge.)
_1863_ and died _August 16th, 1912_. That he was _also_ employed in
(Date of death; cause need not be stated.)
the military or naval service otherwise than as stated above. _As a musician in the Band of_
(Here state what the service was, whether prior or subsequent to
2d Brigade, 1st Division, 6th Corps from Sept. 1st. 1863. to June 33, 1865
that stated above, and the dates at which it began and ended.)
That he was never employed in the military or naval service of the United States after the _23d_
day of _June_ 186 _5_. That she was married under the name of _E._
(Date of soldier's last discharge)
Jennie Van Brunt to said _Charles W. Murdoch_ on
(Name of soldier)
the _5th_ day of _November_ A. D. 185 _7_ by _Rev. Weekes S. Titus,_
at _Fulton, N. J._, there being no legal barrier to such marriage; that she had not
been previously married; that her said husband had not been previously married. (4)

....
(If either had been previously married, so state, and give date of death or divorce of former spouse.)
That she has not remarried since the death of the said _Charles W. Murdoch_
(Name of soldier or sailor.)
That the names and dates of birth of all the children of the soldier, now living, and under sixteen years of
age, are as follows:

..............., born..............., ..., born..............., 18.....

..............., born..............., 18..... ...., born..............., 18.....

..............., born..............., 18..... ...., born..............., 18.....

That she has not abandoned the support of any one of her child. t that they are still under her care or
maintenance. That _A_ prior application for pension has been filed by herself or the soldier. _May 11, 1912._
(A or no.)
Certificate # _565,780. Also under Act of_
(If prior application has been filed, either by soldier or widow, so state giving number assigned to it.)
That she makes this declaration for the purpose of being placed on the pension-roll of the United States,

CLAIMANT'S AFFIDAVIT.

State of _New York_, County of _Oswego_   ss:

In the matter of _The Claim of Charles W. Murdock,_
Bend 2d Brigade, 1st Div. 6th A. C. Act of May 11. 1912.

Personally came before me, a _Notary Public_ in and for the aforesaid County
Notary, Justice or Clerk of Court.

and State, _Charles A. Taylor_, aged _72_ years,
Name of witness.

citizen of the town of _Oswego, 105 E. 7th St. Oswego N.Y._
Post-Office address.   Give Street and No. if in city or town.

County of _Oswego,_, State of _New York_

well known to me to be reputable and entitled to credit, and who, being duly sworn, declares in relation to aforesaid case as follows :

I have this day been shown a family bible
NOTE—Affiants should state how they gain a knowledge of the facts to which they testify.
containing the following record of births in
the following order:

Irene Murdock, was born in Rensselaerville,
Albany Co, March 1, 1797.

Samantha E. Murdock, was born in Scriba, Oswego
Co. N.Y. April 24th, 189.

John Nelson Murdock, was born in Scriba, Oswego Co,
N.Y., Dec. 8, 1820.

James Himes Murdock was born in Scriba, Oswego
Co. N.Y., April 17th, 1823.

Ariel Jerome Murdock, was born at Scriba Oswego Co. N.Y.
Nov, 18, 1827.

Charles W. Murdock, was born in Oswego, N.Y., July 15th
1836. This bible was published, in 1841, by G. Lane and
P.P. Sandford, New York., The record shows no signs of alteration, erasure or interlineations, The writing is
legible and distinct, ink somewhat faded

1 ------------------------------

2 ------------------------------ }   _Charles A. Taylor_
(Signature of Affiant.)

NOTE.—In the execution of papers and evidence, whenever a person or witness signs by mark (†), two persons
who can write must attest the signature by signing their names opposite.
The official before whom papers are executed is _not a competent witness to a mark._

CHAPTER VII

THE SPANISH-AMERICAN WAR

"Spanish-American War: War was declared by Congress 19 April 1898. This war lasted 115 days. Manila in the Philippines surrendered on 13 August 1898; Santiago, Cuba, surrendered 17 July 1898; Puerto Rico surrendered 21 July 1898. As a result of this war the Islands of Philippines, Puerto Rico and Cuba were annexed to the United States as territories. United States paid twenty million dollars to Spain for the Philippine Islands."

A—*Provisions of acts*

Source: *"Federal Military Pensions in the United States"* by William Henry Glasson, Ph.D., Oxford University Press, N.Y. 1918.

Page 145 "Since the general law pension system extends indefinitely forward in its application, there was no need of new invalid-pension legislation for the war with Spain and the Philippine Insurrection. The liberal system of provisions for disabilities originating in actual military service, which had been developed in the thirty-three years since the Civil War, applied at once to the soldier and sailor engaged in the hostilities with Spain."

B—*Bounty land provisions*: none.

C.—*Use and Availability of records*

The War Department has placed a general restriction on its military records that date from 1788, or 75 years. However, the Veterans Administration has a compilation of records, called the "Old War" Index to pension files available through the Microfilm Reading Room, National Archives.

In the book, *Preliminary Inventory of the Records of the Adjutant General's Office*, #17, Washington 1949, page 103, there are several paragraphs that give information pertaining to the *carded* military service records of this war.

A Selected Glossary of Military terms, Abbreviations, etc.

A.G.O.—Adjutant General's Office

Andersonville Prison—(Feb. 1864-Apr. 1865) Georgia—largest and best known of Confederate military prisons. Maximum prisoners: 31,678.

artificer—one who prepares the shells, fuses, grenades, blacksmith, etc.

B.L.W.—Bounty Land Warrant.

battalion—a body of troops arranged for battle varying in number.

battery—two or more pieces of artillery in the field.

cadet—a youth studying for military service.

campaign—a connected series of military operations in war time.

Confederate prisons—(abt. 200,000 prisoners) located at Libby, Macon, Ala; Columbia, S.C. both for officers. Andersonville, Cahaba, Millen, Charleston and Florence for enlisted men. Deserters, spies and political prisoners were kept at Castle Thunder at Richmond, Va. or Salisbury, N.C.

cornet—lowest grade of commissioned officer in calvary, equivalent to ensign in the infantry, his duty being to bear the standard.

dragoon—at one time a kind of mounted infantry or cavalryman.

ensign bearer—one who carries a flag.

expedition—is an enterprise taken by sea or land against an enemy.

farrier—any person who shoes horses, one to a cavalry company.

fort—technically applied to an enclosed work of the higher class of field fortification.

Ind. S.O.—(abbreviation) used in pension files to indicate Indian War Survivor's Original; "Survivor's Certificate" (S.C.); "Widow's Certificate" (W.C.)

invalid pension—is one granted to a soldier on account of wounds or injuries contracted in military service.

manumission—(1790-1860) formal liberation of a slave by means . . . of law.

milice—an old term for militia.

miners—see sappers-miners.

muster roll—a roll or register of the men in each company, troop or regiment.

N.S.O.—"Navy Survivor's Original", also. "N.S.C." and "N.W.C." (see above.)

pension—"specifically, a stated allowance to a person in consideration of past services; payment made to one retired from service; especially a yearly stipend paid by government to retired officers, disabled soldiers, etc.

R.—(abbreviation) meaning "rejected" in Revolutionary War file numbers.

redoubt—a small fort constructed for a temporary purpose.

regiment—a colonel's command—largest permanent association of soldiers.

reservation—land set aside from the public domain for military purposes.

retreat—the retrograde movement of any army . . . away from the enemy.

reville—the beat of the drum (or bugle) about break of day . . . for the soldiers to rise and for the sentinals to forbear challenging.

S.—(abbreviation) "Soldier", "Survivor" in pension file numbers.

S.O.—"Survivor's Original" or "Soldier's Original" (declaration).

saddler—one who works with saddles, at one time, one to a company.

sappers-miners—soldiers belonging to the engineer corps whose business it was to make trenches or saps.

Service pension—"is granted in recognition of military service for a specific length of time, whether a few weeks or months or many years.

tory—(conservative party) the Loyalists were called Tories.

voltigeurs—(Military) from French meaning infantry, sharpshooter.

W.—"Widow" as found in Revolutionary War file numbers.

W.O.—"Widow's Original" as found in pension file numbers.

Whig—(liberal party) a friend and supporter of the American Revolution.

A few selections from the *Historical Geographical Collection* East Reference Room, National Archives, Washington, D.C.

The *Cambridge Modern History Atlas,* edited by Sir. A. W. Ward and others. II ed. N.Y., the Macmillan Co. size abt. 6x9 in. treatise: Europe in particular and the world in general.

The *West Point Atlas of American Wars* vol. I, 1689-1900; vol.. II, 1900-1953. Frederick A. Praiger, Pub. N.Y. 1959. Compiled by the Department of Military Art and Engineering, U.S. Military Academy, West Point, N.Y. Treatise: maps of campaigns (in color) of colonial wars, Revolutionary War, War of 1812, Mexican War, Civil War and Spanish-American War.

Historical Atlas by Wm. R. Shepard, VII ed. Rev. N.Y. Henry Holt & Co. 1929. Treatise: Europe from the beginning, size about 6x9 in., maps in color.

Harper's *Atlas of American History,* (selected from) "The American National Series with map studies, by Dixon Ryan Fox, Ph.D. Harper Bros. N.Y. Maps in color.

Atlas of the Historical Geography of the United States by Charles Oscar Paullin. Carnegie Institute of Washington, Ed. by John K. Wright. Published jointly by the Carnegie Institute of Washington and the American Geographical Society of N.Y. (1932) Treatise: an excellent reference for cartography in U.S., Explorations into the West and Southwest, population studies, boundary disputes within the United States and with Canada, etc.

Atlas of American History by James Truslow Adams, editor, Chas, Schribner's Sons, N.Y. 1943. Treatise: an excellent collection of maps to illustrate military campaigns of all our wars, migrations, early railroads, etc.

Historical Atlas of the United States, by Clifford L. Lord and Elizabeth H. Lord. Henry Holt & Co., N.Y. 1944. Treatise: maps in black and white, more on the economical side than historical. A section shows growth and changes in the District Courts in United States, 1789 to 1861.

Putnam's Historical Atlas, by Ramsey Muir & George Phipip, VI ed. G.P. Putnam's Sons, N.Y. and London, 1927. 96 plates, 229 colored maps, etc.

Campfire and Battlefield, by Rossiter Johnson et al, N.Y. Bryan, Taylor and Co., 1894, 551 pp. Treatise: illustrated history of the campaigns and conflicts of the Great Civil War in America.

A Compendium of the War of the Rebellion, by Frederick H. Dyer, DesMoines, Ia. Dyer Pub. Co. 1908. Treatise: histories of regiments, battles, armies, commands, etc. of the Union Army.

The *War of the Rebellion,* "a compilation of the official records of the Union and Confederate Armies. Published under the direction of the Honorable Elihu Root, Secretary of War, by Brigadier General Fred C. Ainsworth, and others, G/P.O. Washington, 1901. Contains: 130 vols. III series, general index and one volume of atlas information.

"A Special Census of 1890"

Note: This census is of special value for this period in the national history inasmuch as the regular 1890 census of the population was destroyed. This census is available on microfilm at the National Archives. Microfilm Reading Room, second floor, Record Group #15 - M - 123.

The Act of March 1889, establishing a census office in the Department of Interior, provided that the Superintendent of Census, in taking the 11th cesus, should "cause to be taken on a special schedule of inquiry, according to such form as he may prescribe, the names, organizations and length of service of those who have served in the Army, Navy, or Marine Corps of the United States in the War of the Rebellion, and who are survivors at the time of said inquiry and the widows of soldiers, sailors, or marines . . ."

"The work of the enumerators, which was begun on the first Monday of June 1890, was completed by July 1st of that year.

"The original census enumeration was transferred by the Superintendent of Census to the Commissioner of Pensions. (Act 21 April 1894) Under the Act of Congress, 3 July 1930, these schedules were transferred to the Veteran's Administration where they remained until their transfer to the National Archives on March 24, 1943.

". . . for States of Kentucky through Washington, D.C. (included as miscellaneous are California and Kansas and others) bundles #1-53 containing practically all of the schedules for the States of Alabama thru Kansas and approximately half of those for Kentucky appear to have been misplaced or destroyed prior to the transfer of the remaining schedules to the National Archives . . . within each State schedules are arranged numerically by supervisor's districts and thereunder alphabetically by name of county, with the exception of the bundle containing the schedules for Oklahoma and Indian Territories (roll #76) which is arranged numerically by enumeration district.

"Each special census, consisting of four pages contains space for fifty entries. On the upper half of each page are included the name of the veteran, or if he did not survive, the names of both the widow and her deceased husband; the veteran's rank, company, regiment or vessel, date of enlistment, date of discharge, and length of service and street address of each person listed, disability incurred by the veteran and miscellaneous information.

"Persons who enlisted and served under assumed names, and afterwards assumed their lawful names, are listed under their real names followed by their aliases. In a few cases names of Confederate veterans were recorded inadvertantly."

(Note: Obviously, the census pertained only to the Union Army survivors.)

Information Regarding Military Service Records, etc. of
the Confederate States of America.

Note: The information contained in this survey was obtained
by correspondence in February 1961. A letter of inquiry
was sent out that requested information to determine to
what extent any one State provided assistance to its veterans
of the Civil War. Specifically, reference was made to service
pensions, invalid pensions, pensions to widows and dependent children. From the replies received, the following information has been abstracted and presented alphabetically
by States.

ALABAMA—Information furnished by: Department of Pensions and Security, State of Alabama Administrative Building, 64 North Union Street, Montgomery 4, Alabama.

"The State of Alabama does provide for Confederate pensions.
"Alabama does, however, provide Confederate pensions to
certain of the widows of Confederate veterans.
"Alabama has no provision for Conferedate pensions to the
children of a Confederate veteran.
"The official files on service records of Confederate veterans
are maintained by the Alabama Department of Archives and
History located at Washington Avenue, Montgomery, Alabama.
Except for information about service records, we shall be glad
to have you contact this office if additional information is desired
about the Confederate pension program in Alabama."

ARKANSAS—Information furnished by: Department of Public
Welfare, State of Arkansas, Little Rock, Arkansas.

"Yes, Arkansas did provide assistance to veterans of the
Civil War. In fact, the Welfare Department still pays a Con-
federate Only pension and a Confederate Old Age Assistance
grant to widows of soldiers of the Civil War.
"The central archive for this information is: Arkansas
History Commission, Old State House, Little Rock, Arkansas."

FLORIDA—Information furnished by: State Board of Pensions, State of Florida, Tallahassee, Florida.

"The State of Florida has provided over the years pensions to qualified Confederate veterans . . . there are no provisions for children of the Confederacy.

"The State Board of Pensions Office is located in Room 101, Carlton Bldg., Tallahassee, Florida, and it is in this department that records of pensioners who have applied and received pensions are kept . . . also rejected pensions.

"For your information The Church of Jesus Christ of Latter-day Saints of Salt Lake City, microfilmed, some years ago, all the available pension records on file at that time, and it is my understanding that they are on file at Salt Lake City."

GEORGIA—Information furnished by: Department of Archives and History, 1516 Peachtree N.W., Atlanta 9, Georgia.

"The State Division of Confederate Pensions and Records was abolished Jan. 1, 1961 . . . and all historical military and pension records transferred to the Department of Archives and History.

"Military records inherited from the abolished department are filed by regiments and companies. In requesting information please state company, regiment and branch of service; whether Infantry, Cavalry, State Militia, Reserves, etc. It is also helpful to know the county of residence of the soldier *when* he enlisted, rather than *where* he enlisted.

"Pension records are filed as they were originally created by year, beginning in 1879 when the first law for providing for pensions of Georgia Confederate soldiers was passed. Under each year there are separate county files and in these files is listed alphabetically the pensioner's name. We must know: 1. the year the soldier or widow applied for pension. 2. the county in which the pensioner made his or her application.

"*No family statistics are available.* The Archives has no facilities for genealogical research. We can refer you to professional genealogists."

Note: see Miss Lillian Henderson's publication, *Roster of Confederate Soldiers of Georgia,* 1861-1865, in four volumes.

KENTUCKY—Information furnished by: Department of Finance, Commonwealth of Kentucky, Division of Accounts, Frankfort, Kentucky.

"The Commonwealth of Kentucky is paying the needy widows of Confederate veterans a pension. There is no direct program for aid to dependent children of these veterans.

"The best source of information on records may be obtained from the Office of Adjutant General, Department of Military, Record Section, Frankfort, Ky. Other sources: Kentucky Historical Society, Frankfort, Kentucky."

LOUISIANA—Information furnished by: Department of Public Welfare, State of Louisiana, Supervisor of Confederate Pensions, Box 4065, Baton Rouge 4, La.

". . . (in regard to Confederate pensions) please give us, if available to you, his full name, dates of birth and death, place of residence, when he entered service, number of Company and place of residence at time of death. If he left a widow, give us as much information about her as you can.

"We will be glad to forward you a photostatic copy of the record if we can locate it. There is no charge for this service."

MISSISSIPPI—Information furnished by: Department of Archives and History, War Memorial Building, 120 North State Street, Jackson, Mississippi.

(Extracted from booklet, *Research in the Mississippi Department of Archives and History.*)
"There are no official Revolutionary War records on file in the dept.

"War of 1812—a roster of Missippians who served in the War of 1812 with Mexico, is included in the military archives of the Department.

"Civil War—the official Confederate Military Records on file in the Department include more than 80,000 cards containing the name, rank and organization of Mississippi soldiers who served in the Confederate States Army; and some pension applications of Confederate veterans or their widows.

The Department has microfilm and photostat facilities."
Note: see the booklet above for further details about their records.

NORTH CAROLINA—Information furnished by: State of North Carolina, Dept. of the State Auditor, Confederate Pension Bureau, Raleigh, N.C.

(Extracts from their letter and booklet entitled, *Genealogical research in the North Carolina Department of Archives and History*.)

"North Carolina made provision to pension Confederate Soldiers, widows of Confederate soldiers, and colored body-servants who followed their young masters into the army. There is no provision in the law, and never has been, for paying anything to their decendants.

"In 1955 all of the original pension applications . . . there transferred to our Department of Archives and History, Education Building, Raleigh, N.C. Photostat copies of applications and other papers are made by that Department upon request for a fee. The enclosed blue folder will give information that you requested.

(page #6) Pension records: alphabetized pension records for Confederate service by North Carolinians often give considerable information on the individual and are housed in the Archives. These are sometimes filed by name of the veteran, sometimes by the name of the widow. Full name of soldier and county of residence must be furnished when inquiring about Confederate pension records. All other pension applications are on file in the National Archives Records Service, Washington 25, D.C."

OKLAHOMA—Information furnished by: Oklahoma State Library, State Librarian, Oklahoma City 5, Oklahoma.

"Your letter of 18 February 1961, addressed to the Department of Public Welfare, was referred to this Library. The State of Oklahoma gave assistance to its Civil War Confederate Veterans. There are no more living and the records o fthe Confederate Pension Agency have been transferred to the Archives Division of the Oklahoma State Library."

SOUTH CAROLINA—Information furnished by: South Carolina Archives Department, 1430 Senate Street, Columbia 1, S.C.

"The State of South Carolina granted pensions to Confederate veterans and widows, and also granted admittance to the Confederate Home. Daughters were also eligible for admittance to the Home, but not for pensions. Applications for pensions were handled through the Comptroller General's Office and, we think, packaged and filed after a certain number of years. These records have not been transferred to this department. How far back these pension applications are accessible, we do not know.

"A few of the counties paid individual pensions. We have records of some of these on microfilm. If given the name of any indviidual in whom you may be interested, we shall be glad to check our records and see if we find anything concerning him."

TENNESSEE—Information furnished by: Senior Archivist, Tennessee State Library and Archives, Nashville 3, Tennessee.

"Tennessee legislation was passed in 1891 to provide for a Confederate veterans pension, and for the establishment of a home for disabled and indigent ex-Confederate soldiers.

"We can furnish you with photostatic copies of these acts should you so desire . . . the charge would me nominal.

"The pension act has, of course, been amended and liberalized several times down through the years. Widows were also provided for."

TEXAS—Information furnished by: Comptroller of Public Accounts, State of Texas, Austin, Texas.

"In reply to your inquiry, I wish to advise that this State does provide a Confederate pension. There are no veterans presently on our rolls.

"The assistance only extends to their widows and does not include dependent children."

VIRGINIA—Information furnished by: Commonwealth of Virginia, Office of the Comptroller, Chief Pension Clerk, Box 6-N, Richmond 15, Virginia.

"We have been paying pensions to veterans and widows since 1886, and are now paying a small pension of $90.00 per year to dependent needy daughters of Confederate Veterans resident of this State. The last of our Veterans died in March 1959. We have but a few widows of veterans still drawing a pension."

DATES OF CERTAIN WARS, CAMPAIGNS, EXPEDITIONS, EVENTS, etc.

Note: the following pages are taken from the book, *Historical Register* and *Dictionary of the United States Army*, by Francis B. Heitman. "The unofficial work of a private compiler, purchased and published by direction of Congress." Volume II, Washington, Government Printing Office, 1903.

1775-1783   War of the Revolution, 19 April 1775 to 11 April 1783.

1782-1787   Wyoming Valley disturbances, Pennsylvania.

1786-1787   Shays Rebellion, Massachusetts.

1790-1795   War with Northwest Indians, Miamis, Wyandots, Delewares, Pottawattamies, Shawnees, Chippewas, and Ottawas, September 1790 to August 1795.

1791-1794   Whisky Insurrection in Pennsylvania.

1798-1800   War with France, July 1798 to September 30, 1800.

1799   Fries Insurrection in Pennsylvania, Spring of 1799.

1806   Burr Conspiracy.

1806   Sabine Expedition, Louisiana.

1807   Naval appair in Chesapeake Bay, July 9 to August 5, 1807.

1808   Embargo troubles, Lake Champlain, New York.

1811-1813   War with Northwest Indians, November 1811 to October 1813.

1812-1815   War with Great Britain, July 18, 1812 to February 17, 1815.

1812   Florida or Seminole War, August 15 to October 1812.

1813   Peoria Indian War, Illinois, September 19 to October 21, 1813.

1813-1814   Creek Indian War, Alabama, July 27,1813 to August 9, 1814.

1817-1818   Seminole or Florida War, November 20, 1817 to October 31, 1818.

1819   Yellowstone Expedition, July 4 to September 1819.

1823   Campaign against Blackfeet and Arickaree Indians, Upper Missouri River.

1827   Winnebago Expedition, Wisconsin (no fighting) June to Sept. 1827, also called LaFevre War.

1831   Sac and Fox Indian troubles in Illinois.

1832   Black Hawk War, April 26 to September 21, 1832.

1832-1833   Nullification troubles in South Carolina, Nov. 1832 to Feb. 1833.

1833-1839   Cherokee disturbances and removal.

1834   Pawnee Expedition, Indian Territory, June to September 1834.

1835-1836   Toledo War, Ohio and Michigan boundary dispute.

1835-1842   Seminole or Florida War, Nov. 1, 1835 to August 14, 1842.

1836-1837   Creek disturbances in Alabama, May 5, 1836 to September 30, 1837.

1836-1837   Southwestern frontier, Louisiana, Arkansas and Texas (Savine disturbances) no fighting, April 1836 to June 1837.

1837   Osage Indian troubles in Missouri.

1838   Heatherly Indian disturbances in Missouri and Iowa line.

1838   Mormon disturbances in Missouri.

1838-1839   New York, Aroostock, and Canada (Patriot War) disturbances.

1846-1847   Doniphan's Expedition from Santa Fe, New Mexico to Chihuahua, Mexico, November 1846 to February 1847.

1846-1848   Mexican War, April 24, 1846 to May 30, 1848.

1846-1848   New Mexico Expedition, June 30, 1846 to February 13, 1848.

1848   Cayuse War, Oregon volunteers.

1849-1861   Navajo troubles, New Mexico.

1849-1861   Continuous disturbances wih Comanche, Cheyenne, Lipan and Kickapoo Indians in Texas.

1850   Pitt River Expedition, California, April 28 to September 13, 1850.

1851-1852   Yuma Expedition, California, December 1851 to April 1852.

1851-1853   Utah Indian disturbance.

1851-1856   Rogue River, Yakima, Klikitat, Klamath and Salmon River Indian Wars in Oregon and Washington.

1855   Winnas Expedition against Snake Indians, Oregon, May 24 to September 8, 1855.

1855-1856   Sioux Expedition, Nebraska Territory, April 3, 1855 to July 27, 1856.

1855   Yakima Expedition, Washington Territory, October 11 1855 to November 24, 1855.

1855-1856   Cheyenne and Arapaho troubles.

1855-1858	Seminole or Florida War, December 20, 1855 to May 1858.
1856-1858	Kansas Border troubles.
1857	Gila Expedition, New Mexico, April 16 to Sept. 16, 1857.
1857	Sioux Indian troubles in Minnesota and Iowa, March and April 1857.
1857	Mountain Meadow Massacre, Utah, September 11, 1857.
1857-1858	Utah Expedition.
1858	Expedition against Northern Indians, Washington Territory, July 17 to October 17, 1858.
1858	Puget Sound Expedition, Washington Territory, Aug. 10-Sept. 23, 1858.
1858	Spokana, Coeur d'Alene and Paloos Indian troubles in Washington Territory.
1858	Navajo Expedition, New Mexico, Sept. 9 to December 25, 1858.
1858-1859	Wichita Expedition, Indian Territory, Sept. 11, 1858 to Dec. 1859.
1859	Colorado River Expedition, California, Feb. 11 to Apr. 28, 1859.
1859	Pecos Expedition, Texas, April 16 to August 17, 1859.
1859	Antelope Hills Expedition, Texas, June 10 to Sept. 23, 1859.
1859	Bear River Expedition, Utah, June 12 to October 18, 1859.
1859	San Juan imbroglio, Washington Territory, 1859.
1859	John Brown raid, Virginia, November and December 1859.
1859-1860	Cortina troubles in Texas and Mexico border.
1860	Pah-Ute Expedition, California, April 12 to July 9, 1860.
1860	Kiowa and Comanche Expedition, Indian Territory, May 8, Oct. 11, 1860.
1860	Carson Valley Expedition, Utah, May 14 to July 15, 1860.
1860	Attack on and murder of emigrants by Bannock Indians at Salmon Fork, Snake River, Idaho, September 13, 1860.
1860-1861	Navajo Expedition, New Mexico, Sept, 12, 1860 to Feb. 24, 1861.

1861-1890   Apache Indian War and troubles in Arizona and New Mexico.

1861-1866   Civil War, or War of the Rebellion, Apr. 19, 1861 to Aug. 20, 1866. Actual hostilities, however, commenced upon the firing on Fort Sumpter, April 12, 1861 and ceased by the surrender of the Confederate forces under General Kirby Smith, May 1865.

1862   Indian massacres at New Ulm and vicinity, Minn, Aug. 17 to 23, 1862.

1862-1867   Sioux Indian War in Minnesota and Dakota.

1863-1869   War against the Cheyenne, Arapaho, Kiowa, and Comanche Indians in Kansas, Nebraska, Colorado and Indian Territory.

1865-1868   Indian War in southern Oregon and Idaho and Northern California and Nevada.

1865-1866   Fenian raid, New York and Canada border disturbances.

1867-1880   Campaign against Lipsan, Kiowa, Kickapoo and Comanche Indians, and Mexican border disturbances.

1868-1869   Canadian River expedition, New Mexico, Nov. 5, 1868 to Feb. 13, 1869.

1871   Yellowstone Expedition, Aug. 28 to Oct. 25, 1871.

1871   Fenian troubles, Dakota and Manitoba frontier, Sept.-Oct. 1871.

1872   Yellowstone Expedition, Dakota, July 26-Oct. 15, 1872.

1872-1873   Modoc Campaign, Nov 28, 1872 to June 1, 1873.

1873   Yellowstone Expedition, Dakota, June 4, Oct. 4, 1873.

1874-1875   Campaign against Kiowa, Cheyenne and Comanche Indians in the Indian Territory, August 1, 1874 to February 16, 1875.

1874   Sioux Expedition, Wyoming and Nebraska, Feb. 13 to Aug. 19, 1874.

1874   Black Hills Expedition, Dakota, June 20 to Aug. 30, 1874.

1874   Big Horn Expedition, Wyoming, Aug. 13, to Oct. 10, 1874.

1875   Expedition against Indians in eastern Nevada, Sept. 7-27, 1875.

1876   Sioux Expedition, Dakota, May 17 to Sept. 26, 1876.

1876   Powder River Expedition, Wyoming, Nov. 1 to Dec. 31, 1876.

1876-1877   Big Horn and Yellowstone Expedition, Wyoming and Montana, February 17, 1877 to June 13, 1877.

1876-1879   War with Northern Cheyenne and Sioux Indians in Indian Territory, Kansas, Wyoming, Dakota, Nebraska and Montana.

1877   Labor strikes in Pennsylvania and Maryland, July to Oct. 1877.

1878   Bannock and Piute Campaign, May 30 to Sept. 4, 1878.

1878   Ute Expedition, Colorado, Apr. 3 to Sept 9, 1878.

1879   Snake or Sheepeater Indian troubles, Idaho, Aug. to Oct. 1879.

1879-1894   Disturbances of settlers in Indian and Oklahoma Territories, "Oklahoma Boomers" and the Cherokee Strip disturbances.

1879-1880   Ute Indian Campaign in Colorado and Utah, Sept. 21, 1879 to November 8, 1880.

1885   Chinese miner and labor troubles in Wyoming, Sept. and Oct. 1885.

1890-1891   Sioux Indian disturbances in South Dakota, Nov. 1890 to Jan. 1891.

1891-1893   Garza troubles, Texas and Mexican border disturbances, the "Tin Horn War."

1892   Miner disturbances in Idaho, July to Nov. 1892.

1892-1896   Troubles with renegade Apache Indians, under Kidd and Massai in Arizona and Mexican border.

1894   "Industrial Army", "Commonwealers", "Coxyites" and labor disturbances.

1894   Railroad, Pullman and labor strikes, extending from Illionis to Pacific coast, June to August 1894.

1895   Bannock Indian troubles, July and August 1895.

1898-1899   War with Spain, April 21, 1898 to April 11, 1899. Actual hostilities ceased August 13, 1899.

1898   Chippewa Indian disturbances at Leech Lake, Minn., Oct. 1898.

1899-1902   Insurrection in Philippine Islands, February 4, 1899 to July 4, 1902.

1899   Miner disturbances in Idaho, April 29 to October 20, 1899.

1900-1901   Boxer Insurrection in China, murder of Europeans, etc., May 1900 to May 1901.

A SELECTED LIST OF PATRIOTIC AND HEREDITARY SOCIETIES IN U. S.

AZTEC CLUB of 1847
1307 New Hampshire Avenue, Washington 6, D.C.
Founded in 1847—members 170—"Direct male descendants of commissioned officers of the United States armed forces who took part in the Mexican War, also known as the Military Society of the Mexican War."

CATHOLIC WAR VETERANS OF THE U.S.A.
1411-K Street N.W. Washington, D.C.
Founded in 1935—members 120,000 "American veterans of the Catholic Faith." Also, Auxiliary—same address.

NATIONAL SOCIETY OF CHILDREN OF THE AMERICAN
REVOLUTION, 1776 D Street N.W. Washington 6, D.C.
Founded 1895—abt. 18,000 members "Children up to 22 years of age who are lineal descendants of men and women who promoted American independence."

SOCIETY OF THE CINCINNATI
2118 Massachusetts Avenue, N.W. Washington 8, D.C.
Founded in 1783—members 2,000—"Male descendants under the English Law of Primogeniture of officers commissioned in the Continental Army and Navy in the War of the Revolution who gave the required length of service, and of officers in the French Army and Navy."

NATIONAL SOCIETY OF COLONIAL DAMES OF AMERICA
2715 Que Street, Washington 7, D.C.

GENERAL SOCIETY OF COLONIAL WARS
1410-15th Street, N.W. Washington 5, D.C.
Founded 1893—members 3,800—"Male descendants of men who rendered military or civil service to the colonies between 1607 (settlement of Jamestown, Va.) and 1775 (Battle of Lexington)."

NATIONAL SOCIETY, DAUGHTERS OF THE AMERICAN
COLONISTS, 2205 Massachusetts Avenue, N.W. Washington, D.C.
Founded 1921—members 10,000—"Women descended from men and women who gave civil or military service to the colonies prior to the Revolutionary War."

NATIONAL SOCIETY, DAUGHTERS OF THE AMERICAN
REVOLUTION, 1776 D Street, Washington 6, D.C.
Founded 1890—members 186,079—local chapters 2,848.
"Women descended from Revolutionary War veterans."

DAUGHTERS OF THE CINCINNATI
70 East 96th Street, New York 28, N.Y.
Founded 1894—members 356—"Women descendants of the
officers of George Washington Continental Army or Navy."

UNITED DAUGHTERS OF THE CONFEDERACY
328 North Blvd., Richmond 20, Va.
Founded 1894—members 35,000— local groups 1,000—
"Women descendants of Confederate veterans of the Civil War."

NATIONAL SOCIETY SONS OF THE AMERICAN REVOLU-
TION (SAR), 2412 Massachusetts Avenue, N.W. Washington 8, D.C.
Founded 1889—members 20,000—"Descendants of men who
actively participated in the Revolutionary War."

GENERAL SOCIETY SONS OF THE REVOLUTION (SR)
Fraunces Tavern, 54 Pearl Street, New York 4, N.Y.
Founded 1890—members 6,000—"Descendants of either par-
ents side of veterans of the American forces who served in the
American Revolution of 1776."

SONS OF UNION VETERANS OF THE CIVIL WAR
P. O. Box 457, Trenton 3, New Jersey.
Founded 1881—members 8,000—"Male descendants of vet-
erans of the Union Army of the Civil War."

NAVAL & MILITARY ORDER OF THE SPANISH—AMERI-
CAN WAR, 453-4th Avenue, South, St. Petersburg 1,
Florida.
Founded 1899—members 260—"Former commissioned offi-
cers of the United States armed forces who served in the Spanish-
American War and enlisted men who served during that period
and were later commissioned."

UNITED SPANISH WAR VETERANS
40 G Street, N.W. Washington 2, D.C.
Founded 1899—members 33,000—"Veterans of war with
Spain who served between April 21, 1898 and July 4, 1902."

GENERAL SOCIETY OF THE WAR OF 1812
    3311 Columbia Pike, Lancaster, Pa.
    Founded 1814—members 983—"Male descendants of veterans of War of 1812."

MILITARY SOCIETY OF THE WAR OF 1812
    Seventh Regiment Armory, 643 Park Avenue, New York 21, N.Y.
    Founded 1790—members 225—"Hereditary society of descendants of any defender of the country in the American Revolution and the War of 1812 and those who have served honorably in the Armies and Navies of the U.S."

SOCIETY OF THE WAR OF 1812 in the Commonwealth of
    Pennsylvania, 6 Penn Center Plaza, Room 1036, Philadelphia 3, Pa.
    Founded—1854—members 235—"A patriotic organization."

Source: *Encyclopedia of Associations*, III ed. (1961) Gale Research Co., Book Tower—Detroit 26, Michigan.

DAUGHTERS OF THE DEFENDERS OF THE REPUBLIC,
    U.S.A., 600 West 162 Street, New York 32, N.Y.
    Founded 1927—*"Women Descendants of American War Veterans."*

NATIONAL SOCIETY OF UNITED STATES DAUGHTERS
    OF 1812, 1461 Rhode Island Avenue N.W., Washington 5, D.C.
    Founded 1892—members 3,850. "Women descendants of those who rendered civil, military or naval service during the years 1784-1815."

NATIONAL SOCIETY COLONIAL DAUGHTERS OF THE
    17th CENTURY, 1600 Bath Avenue, Ashland, Kentucky.

NATIONAL SOCIETY, DAUGHTERS OF THE UNION—1861-
    1865. 2516 North Alabama Street, Indianapolis 5, Indiana.
    Founded 1912—members 700—"Women descendants of Union Army veterans or of women whose service to the North was recognized by the government."

NATIONAL SOCIETY, DAUGHTERS OF UTAH PIONEERS
    300 North Main Street, Salt Lake City, Utah.
    Founded 1901—members 35,000—"Descendants of Utah Pioneers."

ORDER OF THE FOUNDERS & PATRIOTS OF AMERICA
c/o Federal Hall Memorial, 15 Pine Street, New York 5, N.Y.

Founded 1896—members 900—"Men who are lineal descendants in the male line of either of their parents from an ancestor who settled in any of the colonies now included in the United States, prior to May 13, 1657, and those whose intermediate descendants in the same line adhered as a patriot during he American Revolution."

LADIES OF THE GRAND ARMY OF THE REPUBLIC
7602-N.E. 105th Avenue, Portland, Oregon.

Founded 1885—members 10,560. "Relatives of Union veterans and nurses of the Civil War."

UNITED INDIAN WAR VETERANS, U.S.A.
507 Haight Street, San Francisco 17, California.

Founded 1912—members 150—"Veterans who served in campaigns against American Indians, 1817 to 1906; their dependants and blood kin, both male and female."

DAMES OF THE LOYAL LEGION OF THE UNITED STATES
1900 F Street N.W. Washington 6. D.C.

Founded 1899—members 200—"Women descendants of commissioned officers of the Union Army during Civil War."

MILITARY ORDER OF THE LOYAL LEGION OF THE UNITED STATES, 1805 Pine Street, Philadelphia 3, Pa.
Founded 1865—members 1,300—"Male descendants of commissioned officers serving in the Union Army during the Civil War, and descendants of brothers and sisters of such officers."

MEXICAN WAR VETERANS
P.O. Box 33035—Indianapolis 3, Indiana.

"Veterans of Mexican Border Campaign."

BIBLIOGRAPHY PERTAINING TO PUBLISHED LISTS OF SERVICEMEN AND PENSIONERS IN AMERICA

GENERAL:

WALDENMAIER, NELLIE PROTSMAN, ed. *Some of the Earliest Oaths of Allegiance to the United States of America* (edited by) Nellie Protsman Waldenmaier. Lancaster, Pa. (by Lancaster Press. Inc.) 1944, 93p-23½cm. LC-E209.W3.

KNOX, Capt. JOHN D. 1778. *An Historical Journal of the Campaigns in North America for the Years 1757, 1758, 1759, and 1760;* Toronto, The Champlain Society, 1914-16. 3v.-25cm. LC-E299.K76.

DRAKE, SAMUEL ADAMS, 1833-1905. *The Border Wars of New England, commonly called King William's and Queen Anne's Wars;* New York, C. Schribner's Sons. 1897. 305p-19½cm. LC-E206.D76.

PENHALLOW, SAMUEL, 1665-1726. *The History of the Wars of New England with the Eastern Indians,* or a narrative of their continued perfidy and cruelty, from the 10th of August, 1703, to the peace renewed 13th of July 1713. 129p.-23cm. LC-E197.P392 .

—A List of the General and Staff Officers, and of the Officers in the Several Regiments Serving in North America under the command of His Excellency General Sir William Howe, K. B. with the Dates of Their Commissions as They Rank in Each Corps and in the Army. New York, Printed by J. Rivington, 1778. 68p.-24cm. LC-E267.L78.

DE LANCEY'S BRIGADE (Loyalist) 1776-1778. *Orderly Book of the Three Battalions of Loyalists commandell by Brigadier-General Oliver De Lancey, 1776-1778;* to which is appended a list of New York loyalists in the city of New York during the War of the Revolution—comp. by William Kelby. New York, printed for the New York Historical Society, 1917. 147p.-25½cm. LC-E277.6.D3D3.

ESTES, CLAUD, comp. *List of Field Officers, Regiments and Battalions in the Confederate States Army,* 1861-1865. Macon, Ga., The J. W. Burke Company, 1912. 76p.-24cm. LC-E548.#79.

MACDONELL, JOHN ALEXANDER. 1851. *Sketches Illustrating the Early Settlement and History of Glengarry in Canada,* relating principally to the Revolutionary War of 1775-83, the War of 1812-14 and the Rebellion of 1837-8, and the Services of the King's Royal Regiment of New York, the 84th or Royal Highland Emigrant Regiment. the Royal Canadian Volunteer Regiment of Foot, the Glengarry Fencible or British Highland Regiment, the Glengarry Light Infantry Regiment, and the Glengarry Militia. By J. A. Macdonell, Montreal, W. Foster, Brown & Co., 1893. 337p-25cm. LC-F1059.G5M2.

REVOLUTIONARY WAR

BRUMBAUGH, GAIUS MARCUS, 1862. *Revolutionary War Records;* Washington, D.C. 1936. 26½cm. LC-E255.B85.

FORD, WORTHINGTON CHAUNCEY, 1858-1941, comp. *British Officers Serving in America.* 1754-1774. Comp. from the "Army Lists" by Worthington Chauncey Ford; Boston (Press of D. Clapp & Son) 1894. 108p-25½cm. LC-E299.F695.

RAY, ALEXANDER. *Officers of the Continental Army, who Served to the End of the War.* and acquired the right to commutation pay and bounty land; also Officers killed in the service. Comp. by Alexander Ray. Washington. J. and G. S. Gideon, printers, 1849. 44p-22½cm. LC-E255.R26.

HEITMAN, FRANCIS BERNARD. 1838-1926. *Historical Register of Officers of the Continental Army During the War of the Revolution, April 1775 to Dec. 1783;* Washington, D.C. 525p-25cm. LC-E255.H472.

KELBY, ROBERT HENDRE, 1847-1927. *Addenda to Heitman's Historical Register of Officers of the Continental Army during the War of the Revolution. April 1775 to December 1783.* 6p.25cm. LC-E255.H49.

MEXICAN WAR:

U.S. Adjutant-General's Office. *Military Forces Employed in the Mexican War.* 34p-25cm. LC-E409.U55.

ROBARTS, WILLIAM HUGH. *Mexican War Veterans* A complete roster of the regular and volunteer troops in the war between the United States and Mexico, from 1846 to 1848. Compiled from official sources by Wm. Hugh Robarts. Washington, D.C., Brentano's 1887. 80p-23cm. LC-E409.R62.

CIVIL WAR:

U. S. Adjutant-General's Office. *Official Army Register of the Volunteer Force of the United States Army for the Years* 1861, '62, '63, '64, '65; Washington, 1865067. 8v. plates.-20½cm. LC-E494.U538.

U. S. Adjutant-General's Office. *Official Army Register for* 1861-(1865) Washington, Adjutant General's Office, 1861-65. 7v.-21½cm. LC-U11.U4 1861-1865.

SMITH, GEORGE B. of Chicago, comp. *Official Army List of the Volunteers of Illinois, Indiana, Wisconsin, Minnesota, Michigan, Iowa, Missouri. Kansas, Nebraska, and Colorado;* Chicago; 1862. 176p-18cm. LC-E494.S64.

LISTING BY STATES:

ALABAMA. Adjutant-General's Office. (*Muster Rolls of Alabama Volunteers in the Spanish American War of* 1898. Montgomery, 1899) 36p-22cm LC-E726.A3A3.

ALABAMA. Dept. of Archives & History. *Revolutionary Soldiers in Alabama.* Montgomery, Ala. The Brown Printing Company, printers. 1911. 131p-24cm. LC-F321.A13 no. 5.

CALIFORNIA. Adjutant-General's Office *Records of California men in the War of the Rebellion,* 1861 to 1867. Revised and compiled by Brig.-Gen. Richard H. Orton. Sacramento, State Office, 1890. 887p-23½cm. LC-E497.3.C16.

BACHELDER, HORACE W. *Illustrated Roster of California Volunteer Soldiers in the War with Spain,* 87p-25½cm. LC-E726.C1B12.

CONNECTICUT, Adjutant-General's Office. *Record of Service of Connecticut Men in the* I.—*War of the Revolution.* II.—*War of* 1812. III.—*Mexican War.* Lockwood & Brainard Company, printers 1889. 779p.-30½cm. LC-E263.C5C5.

CONNECTICUT HISTORICAL SOCIETY, Hartford. *Rolls of Connecticut Men in the French and Indian War,* 1775-1762. Hartford, Connecticut Historical Society, 1903-05. 2v. 25cm. LC-E199.C75.

CONNECTICUT INFANTRY. Waterbury's Regiment, 1776. *A Complete Roster of Colonel David Waterbury Jr.'s Regiment of Connecticut Volunteers.* 20p.-24cm. LC-E263. C5C67.

SHEPARD, JAMES. 1838-1926. *Connecticut Soldiers in the Pequot War of* 1637. 32p.-22½Cm. LC-E83.63.S54.

CONNECTICUT. Adjutant-General's Office. *Record of Service of Connecticut Men in the Army, Navy, and Marine Corps of the United States in the Spanish-American War, Philippine Insurrection and China Relief Expedition From April 21, 1898, to July 4, 1904.* Hartford, Conn., press of the Case Lockwood & Brainard Company, 1919. 222p.-31cm. LC-E726.C7C68.

CONNECTICUT. Adjutant General's Office. *Record of Connecticut Men in the War of Rebellion,* 1861-1865; *Spanish-American War, Philippine Insurrection, China Relief Expedition:* 1898-1904; errata. Hartford. 1936. 27cm. LC-E499.3.C788.

CONNECTICUT HISTORICAL SOCIETY. Hartford. *Lists and Returns of Connecticut men in the Revolution.* 1775-1783. Hartford, Connecticut Historical Society, 1909, 489p-25cm. LC-E263.C5C54.

CONNECTICUT. Adjutant-General's Office. *Record of Service of Connecticut Men in the Army and Navy of the United States During the War of the Rebellion.* Hartford, Conn., press of the Case, Lockwood & Brainard Company, 1889. 1071p.-30½cm. LC

CONNECTICUT. Adjutant-General's Office. *Roster of Connecticut Volunteers Who Served in the War Between the United States and Spain* 1898-1899. Hartford, Conn., The Case, Lockwood & Brainard Co., 1899. 42p-23cm. LC-F726.C7C7.

DELAWARE. Public Archives Commission. *Delaware Archives.* Published by the Public Archives Commission of Delaware by authority. Wilmington, Del., 1911. 29cm. LC-F161.D29.

WARD, CHRISTOPHER, 1868. *The Delaware Continentals, 1776-1783,* by Christopher L. Ward. Wilmington, Del., The Historical Society of Delaware, 1941 620p.-24cm. LC-E263.D3W3.

FLORIDA. Board of State Institutions. *Soldiers of Florida in the Seminole Indian, Civil and Spanish-American Wars.* 368p.-24½cm. LC-E558.3.F63.

SMITH, GEORGE GILMAN, 1836. *The Story of Georgia and the Georgia people, 1732 to* 1860. Macon, Ga., G. G. Smith, 1900. 634p-23½cm. LC-F286.S66.

GEORGIA. Dept of Archives and History. *Revolutionary Soldiers' Receipts for Georgia Bounty Grants.* Issued by the Georgia State Department of Archives and History. Foote and Davies Company, 1928. 2-85p.-31cm.

GEORGIA CALVARY. Georgia Hussars, 1736. *Roll of Officers and Members of the Georgia Hussars and of the Cavalry Companies.* Savannah, Ga. The Morning News, 1906. 560p.-24cm. LC-UA155.A6 1905.

ILLINOIS. Military and Naval Dept. *Records of the Services of Illinois Soldiers in the Black Hawk War.* 343p.-23½cm. LC-E83.83.I29.

ILLINOIS. Military and Naval Dept. *Record of the Services of Illinois Soldiers in the Black Hawk War.* 1831-32, and in the Mexican War, 1846-8 9v-22cm. LC-UA172.A2.

——*Annual Report of the Adjutant General of the State of Illinois,* Springfield: Baker and Phillips, printers 1863 (Civil War) 383 p. LC# ....

INDIANA. Adjutant General's Office. *Record of Indiana Volunteers in the Spanish-American War 1898-1899;* Indianapolis, W. B. Burford, 1900. 368p-23½cm. LC-E726.I3I3.

INDIANA. Adjutant-General's Office. *Indiana in the Mexican War;* Indianapolis, W. B. Burford 1908. 496p-23½cm. LC-E4095.1713.

——*Report of the Adjutant General of the State of Indiana.* vols.1-8 (Indiana in the War of the Rebellion) Indianapolis, Alex H. Conner, state printer 1869. LC.............

——*Report of the Adjutant General and Acting Quartermaster General of Iowa.* Jan. 1, 1863, vols 1-2 (Civil War) Des Moines. F. W. Palmer, printer, 1863.

——*Report of Nathaniel B. Baker,* Adjutant General of Iowa to Hon. Wm. M. Stone, Governor of Iowa. Jan. 1, 1867-Jan. 14, 1868. Des Moines, F. W. Palmer, state printer 1868. 113p.

IOWA. Adjutant-General's Office. *Iowa Soldiers in the War of the Rebellion,* 1908-11. LC-E507.3.164.

IOWA. Adjutant-General's Office. *Roster and Record of Iowa Soldiers in the War of the Rebellion,* together with historical sketches of volunteer organizations, 1861-1866. Des Moines, E. H. English, state printer. 1908-11. 6v.-23cm. LC.............

——*Report of the Adjutant General of the State of Kansas* 1861-65—vol. I. Topeka, Kansas State Ptg. Co. 1896. 654p & appendix 294.

——*13th Biennial Report of the Adjutant General of the State of Kansas* 1901-02 Topeka, W. Y. Morgan, state printer 1902. 268p.

——*Report of the Adjutant General of the State of Kansas for the Year* 1864, Leavenworth: P. H. Hubbell & Co. Book & Job Printers 1865. 714p.

KANSAS. Adjutant General's Office. *Kansas Troops in the Volunteer Service of the United States in the Spanish and Philippine Wars;* Topeka. W. Y. Morgan, state printer, 1900. 261p.-23½cm. LC-E726.K2K2.

KENTUCKY. Adjutant-General's Office. *Report of the Adjutant General of the State of Kentucky.* Soldiers of the War of 1812; Frankfort, Ky., E. P. Johnson, public printer, 1891. 370p-31x25cm. LC-E359.5K5K3.

Report of the Adjutant General of the State of Kentucky, vols. I & II, 1861-1866, Frankfort, Ky.-1866, John H. Harvey, public printer.

Annual Report of the Adjutant General of the State of Louisiana for the Year Ending Dec. 31, 1889; New Orleans. E. Marchand, state printer, 1890. 101p.

Annual Report of the Adjutant General of the State of Maine for the Year Ending Dec. 31. 1861. Augusta: Stevens & Sayward, printers to the state, 1862.

Adjutant General's Office, Maine. *Returns of the Desertions, Discharges & Deaths in Maine Regiments.* Jan., Feb., Mar., 1863. 250p.

Annual Report of the Adjutant General of the State of Maine for the Year Ending Dec. 31, 1862. Augusta: Stevens & Sayward, printers to the state 1863. Ibed: 1864-65-66.

SOCIETY OF COLONIAL WARS. Maine. *Register of the Officers and Members of the Society of Colonial Wars in the State of Maine,* 1905. 180p-24½cm. LC-E186.3.M22.

MARYLAND LOYALISTS REGIMENT. *Orderly Book of the "Maryland Loyalists Regiment" June 18th,* 1778, *to October 12th* 1778. Brooklyn, N.Y. Historical Printing Club, 1891. 111p.123½cm. LC-E277.6.M2M2.

MARYLAND HISTORICAL SOCIETY. *Muster Rolls and Other Records of Service of Maryland Troops in the American Revolution,* 1775-1783; Baltimore, Md. Historical Society, 1900. 736p-28cm. LC-F176.A67.

RILEY. HUGH RIDGELY. *Roster of the Soldiers and Sailors Who Served in Organizations From Maryland During the Spanish-American War;* Baltimore, W. J. C. Dulany Co., 1901. 51p.-24cm. LC-E726.M35R5.

NEWMAN, HARRY WRIGHT, 1894-comp. *Maryland Revolutionary Records;* data obtained from 3,050 pension claims and bounty land applications, including 1,000 marriages of Maryland soldiers and a list of 1,200 proved services of soldiers and patriots of other states, by Harry Wright Newman; Washington, published by the compiler, 1938. 155p-23½cm. LC F185.N48.

MARINE, WILLIAM MATTHEW, b. 1843. *The British Invasion of Maryland,* 1812-1815, with an appendix, containing eleven thousand names by Louis Henry Dielman. Baltimore, Society of the War of 1812 in Maryland, 1913. 519p-23½cm.

History & Roster of Maryland Volunteers—War of 1861-65 vol. I (1898) Guzzenheimer Weil & Co., Baltimore, Md. vol. I, 831p, vol. II, 285p.

BODGE, GEORGE MADISON. *Soldiers in King Philip's War.* Containing lists of the soldiers of Massachusetts colony, who served in the Indian War of 1675-1677. 369p-20½cm. LC-E83.B658.

ROBINSON, GEORGE FREDERICK. 1860-comp. *Watertown Soldiers in the Colonial Wars and the American Revolution,* compiled by G. Frederick Robinson and Albert Harrison Hall. Watertown, Mass., The Historical Society of Watertown, 1939. 75p-24½cm. LC-F74.W33R63.

MASSACHUSETTS. Adjutant General's Office. *Records of the Massachusetts Volunteer Militia Called Out by the Governor of Massachusetts to Suppress a Threatened Invasion During the War of 1812-14.* Boston, Wright & Potter Printing Co., 1913. 448p-31½cm. LC-E359.5.M3.

MASSACHUSETTS. Secretary of the Commonwealth. *Massachusetts Soldiers and Sailors of the Revolutionary War.* Boston, Wright and Potter Printing Co., state printers, 1896-1908. 17v-27cm. LC-E263.M4M4.

NEBRASKA. Secretary of State. *Roster of Soldiers, Sailors, and Marines of the War of 1812, the Mexican War, and the War of the Rebellion,* residing in Nebraska, December 1, 1897. Lincoln, Neb., J. North & Co., printers 1898. 426p-22½cm. LC-UA39.N2A3-1897.

NEW HAMPSHIRE. *Roll of New Hampshire Men at Louisburg.* Cape Breton, 1745. Concord, 1896. 63p-25cm. LC-E198.N51.

THE NEW HAMPSHIRE *Register, and United States Calendar.* Portsmouth; 1772-1817; Concord (1818-72) 15½cm. LC-JK2931.

GILMORE, GEORGE CLINTON, d. 1912, comp. *Roll of New Hampshire Soldiers at the Battle of Bennington, August* 16, 1777. Manchester, N. H., Printed by J. B. Clarke, 1891. 55p-26cm. LC-E241.B4G4.

HAMMOND, ISAAC WEARE. *Rolls of the Soldiers in the Revolutionary War.* Concord, N.H. P. B. Cogswell, state printer 1885-89. 4v.-23cm. LC-F31N42 vol. 14-17.

NEW JERSEY. Adjutant-General's Office. *Official Register of the Officers and Men of New Jersey in the Revolutionary War.* Trenton, N.J., W. T. Nicholson & Co., printers, 1872. 878p-24cm. LC-E263.N5N55.

McNALLY, BERNARD, comp. *Soldiers and Sailors of New Jersey in the Spanish-American War.* Newark, N.J. B. McNally, 1898. 46p-26cm. LC-E726.N4M1.

STRYKER, WILLIAM SCUDDER, 1838-1900. *The New Jersey Volunteers (Loyalists) in the Revolutionary War.* By William S. Stryker. Trenton. N.J., Naar, Day & Naar, printers, 1887. 67p-25cm. LC-E277.6.N5S92.

NEW JERSEY. Adjutant-General's Office. *Records of Officers and Men of New Jersey in Wars 1791-1815.* Trenton, N.J., State Gazette Publishing Co., printers, 1909. 411p.-30½cm. LC-E359.5.N4N3.

NEW YORK HISTORICAL SOCIETY. *Muster Rolls of New York Provincial Troops.* 1755-1764. 621 p.-25cm. LC-F116.N63.

NEW YORK HISTORICAL SOCIETY. *Muster and Pay Rolls of the War of the Revolution.* 1775-1783. 2v.-25cm. LC-F116.N63.

CLARK, FRANCIS D. *The First Regiment of New York Volunteers in the Mexican War.* 94p-24cm. LC-E409.C59.

NEW YORK (State) Adjutant General's Office. *Index to New York in the Spanish-American War*. Albany; J. B. Lyon Company, printers 1914. 448p.-23cm. LC-E726. N5N6.

NEW YORK (State) Secretary of State. *A List of the Names of Persons to Whom Military Patents Have Issued Out of the Secretary's Office, and to Whom Delivered*. Francis Childs and John Swaine, printers to the state, 1793. 25p-34cm: LC-UB674N7A5-1793.

NORTH CAROLINA. Adjutant General's Dept. *Roster of the North Carolina Volunteers in the Spanish-American War*, 1898-1899. Prepared under the direction of the Adjutant-General. Raleigh, Edwards & Broughton and E. M. Uzzell, state printers, 1900. 131p-24½cm. LC-#726.N8N8.

NORTH CAROLINA. Adjutant-General's Dept. *Muster Rolls of the Soldiers of the War of 1812. Detached from the Militia of North Carolina in 1812 and 1814*. Raleigh. printed by C. C. Raboteau, 1841. 140p.-22½cm. LC-E359.5.N7N7.

DAUGHTERS OF THE AMERICAN REVOLUTION. North Carolina. *Roster of the Soldiers from North Carolina in the American Revolution*. 700p.-23½cm. LC-E263.N8D17.

NORTH CAROLINA. *The State Records of North Carolina*. Goldsboro, N.C., Nash Brothers, printers; 1886-1907. 26v.-27½cm. LC-F251.N6.

OHIO. Roster Commission. *Official Roster of the Soldiers of the State of Ohio in the War of the Rebellion*, 1861-1866. Akron, Werner Co., 1886-95. 12v.-25½cm. LC-E525.3.038.

OHIO. Adjutant-General's dept. *The Official Roster of Ohio Soldiers in the War with Spain*, 1898-1899. (Columbus, O., E. T. Miller Co.) 1916. 960p.-24cm. LC-E726.03025.

OHIO. Adjutant-General's Dept. *Roster of Ohio Soldiers in the War of 1812*. Columbus, O., Press of The Edward T. Miller Co., 1916. 157p.-24cm. LC-E359.5.0203.

OREGON. Adjutant-General's Office. *The Official Records of the Oregon Volunteers in the Spanish War and Philippine Insurrection*, comp. by Brigadier-Gen. C. U. Gantenbein. Adjutant General. Salem, Or., W. H. Leeds, state printer, 1902. 700p.-24cm. LC-DS68.3.06A2.

EGLE, WILLIAM HENRY. *Journals and Diaries of the War of the Revolution, with Lists of Officers and Soldiers*. 1775-1783. Harrisburg, E. K. Meyers, state printer, 1893. 784p.-21½cm. LC-F146.P41 2d ser., vol. 15.

PENNSYLVANIA. Adjutant-General's Office. *Record of Pennsylvania Volunteers in the Spanish-American War*, 1898. Harrisburg; W. S. Ray, state printer, 1900. 952p.125cm. LC-E726..P4P4.

EGLE, WILLIAM HENRY, 1830-1901, ed. *Muster Rolls of the Navy and Line Militia and Rangers*, 1775-1783. With list of pensioners. 1818-1832. (Harrisburg) W. S. Ray, state printer, 1898. 830p.-21½cm. LC-F146.P41 3d ser., vol. 23.

Muster Rolls of the Pennsylvania Volunteers in the War of 1812-1814. Harrisburg, L. S. Hart, state printer, 1880. 850p.-22cm. LC-F146.P41 2d ser., vol. 12.

PENNSYLVANIA (Colony) *Officers and Soldiers in the Service of the Province of Pennsylvania*. 1744-1764. In Pennsylvania Archives. Harrisburg, 1876. 21cm. 2d Ser., v. 2, p(487-615) LC-F146.P41.

Expenditures by the State of Pennsylvania on Account of the United States—1812-14. (In Pennsylvania Archives. Harrisburg, 1907. 21½cm. 6th ser., v. 10. P. 1-246) LC-F146.P41. 6th ser. v. 10. E359.5.)3E9.

Miscellaneous Papers. 1812-1814. Drafted Troops. 1812-1814. Harrisburg, Pa. Harrisburg Publishing Company, 1907. 924p.21½cm. LC-F146.P41. 6th ser. vol. 9. E359.5.P3M6.

Muster Rolls, etc., (1743-1787) Harrisburg, Pa., Harrisburg Publishing Co., state printer, 1906. 10v.-21½cm. (Pennsylvania Archives; fifth series, vol. I-VIII; sixth series, vol. I-II) LC-F146.P41 6th ser., vol. 15. pt. 1-2 E263.P4M7 Index.

Muster Rolls of the Pennsylvania Volunteers, in the War of 1812-1814, with pay rolls, etc. Harrisburg, Pa., Harrisburg Pub. Co., state printer, 1907. 964p.-21cm. LC-F146.P41 6th ser., vol. 7. E359.5.P3M9.

RHODE ISLAND. *Rhode Island in the War with Spain*. Providence, E. L. Freeman & Sons, printers to the state, 1900. 417p-24cm. LC-E726.R4R36.

SOCIETY OF COLONIAL WARS. Rhode Island. *The Muster Rolls of Three Companies Enlisted by the Colony of Rhode Island in May, 1746, for an Expedition Against Canada Proposed by Great Britain*. 3-5p-23½cm. LC-198.S67.

SOCIETY OF COLONIAL WARS. Rhode Island. *Nine Muster Rolls of Rhode Island Troops Enlisted During the Old French War;* Providence, printed by the Standard Printing Co. (1915) 3-54p.-24cm. LC-E199.S69.

CHAPIN, HOWARD MILLAR. 1887. *Rhode Island in the Colonial Wars.* A list of Rhode Island soldiers & sailors in the Old French & Indian War, 1755-1762 by Howard M. Chapin. Providence. Printed for the society, 1918. 155p.-24cm. LC-E199.C46.

CHAPIN, HOWARD MILLAR. 1887.*Rhode Island in the Colonial Wars.* A list of Rhode Island soldiers & Sailors in King George's War, 1740-1748. Providence, printed for the society, 1920. 38p.-23½cm. LC-F82.C48.

SOUTH CAROLINA. Treasury. *Stub Entries to Indents Issued in Payment of Claims Against South Carolina Growing Out of the Revolution.* Columbia, printed for the Historical Commission of South Carolina by the State Co., 1910. v. 24cm. LC-E263. S7S7.

ERVIN, SARA (SULLIVAN) ed. *South Carolinians in the Revolution, with Service Records and Miscellaneous data, also Abstracts of Wills,* Laurens County (Ninety-Six District) 1775-1855. Ypsilanti. Mich. 1949. 217p.-24cm. LC-263.S7E78.

SOUTH CAROLINA INFANTRY 3d Regt. 1775-1781. *An Order Book of the Third Regiment, South Carolina Line, Continental Establishment, December 23, 1776-May 2, 1777.* Edited by A. S. Salley. Columbia, printed for the Historical Commission of South Carolina by the State Co., 1942. 44p.-24cm. LC-E263.S7S62.

GAINES, GEORGE TOWNS. *Fighting Tennesseans,* by George Towns Gaines. Kingsport Press, 1931. 127p.-23½cm. LC-F435.G23.

BATTERY, GEORGE MAGRUDER, 1887. *The Tennessee "Bee Hive"; or Early* (1778-1791) *N.C. Land Grants in the Volunteer State, being an Index with Some* 3,100 *Names of Revolutionary Soldiers and Settlers Who Participated in the Distribution of More Than 5,000,000 Acres of Land.* Washington, 1949. 68p.-30cm. LC-E255.B27.

CARTWRIGHT, BETTY GOFF COOK, comp. *North Carolina Land Grants in Tennessee,* 1778-1791. Compiled by Betty Goff Cook Cartwright and Lillian Johnson Gardner. 199p.-24cm. LC-E255.C33.

DAUGHTERS OF THE AMERICAN REVOLUTION. Tennessee. *Membership Roster and Soldiers,* 1894-1960. Compiled by Edythe Rucker Whitley, registrar, Tennessee Society. 1690p.-29cm. LC-202.5.T22.

ALLEN, PENELOPE JOHNSON, comp. *Tennessee Soldiers in the Revolution;* a roster of soldiers living during the Revolutionary War in the counties of Washington and Sullivan. Bristol, Tennessee. The King Printing Company 1935. 71p.-23½cm. LC-E263 N8A37.

TYLER, DANIEL, b. 1816. *A Concise History of the Mormon Battalion in the Mexican War.* 1846-1847. By Sergeant Daniel Tyler. Salt Lake City, 1881. 376p.-23cm. LC-E409.5.I 72T9.

A. PRENTISS. *The History of the Utah Volunteers in the Spanish-American War and in the Philippine Islands.* A complete history of all the military organizations in which Utah men served. W. F. Ford, publisher: A. Prentiss, editor. (Salt Lake City. 1900) 430p.-22½cm. LC-DS683.U5P9.

MAYBE, CHARLES R. *The Utah Batteries; A History.* Salt Lake City, 1900. 130p.-23cm. LC-DS683.U5M2.

COOKE, PHILIP ST. GEORGE, 1809-1895. *Exploring Southwestern Trails,* 1846-1854, Glendale, Calif., The Arthur H. Clark Company. 1938. 383p.-24½cm. LC-F786.C78.

VERMONT. Adjutant and Inspector General's Office. *Roster of Soldiers in the War of* 1812-14. (St. Albans, The Messenger Press) 1933. 274p.-23½cm. LC-E359.5.V3V32.

CLARK, BYRON N. ed. *A List of Pensioners of the War of* 1812, Burlington and Boston, Research Publication Company, 1904. 171p.-24cm. LC-E859.4.062.

Roster of Soldiers in the War of 1812-14 by Herbert T. Johnson. The Adjutant General 1933. Messenger Press, St. Albans, Vt. 474p.

SOCIETY OF THE CINCINNATI. Virginia. *Officers of the Virginia Forces in the Revolutionary War at Present Represented in the Society of the Cincinnati in the State of Virginia,* with names of their representatives, October 29, 1922. Richmond, 1912. 11p.-27x21cm. LC-E263.V8S6.

MCALLISTER. JOSEPH THOMPSON, 1866-1927. *Virginia Militia in the Revolutionary War;* McAllister's data by J. T. McAllister. Hot Springs. Va., McAllister Publishing Co. (1913).

NOTTINGHAM, STRATTON, comp. *Revolutionary Soldiers and Sailors from Northampton County, Virginia;* (Onancock, Va., 1929) 71p.-26cm. LC-F232.N85N93.

GWATHMEY, JOHN HASTINGS, 1886—*Historical Register of Virginians in the Revolution; Soldiers, Sailors, Marines,* 1775-1783 by John H. Gwathmey; introduction by Dr. H. J. Eckenrode, Richmond, Va., The Dietz Press, 1938, 872p-23½cm. LC-E263. V8G9.

VIRGINIA. Auditor of Public Accounts. *Muster Rolls of the Virginia Militia in the War of 1812,* being a supplement to the Pay Rolls printed and distributed in 1851. Richmond, Va., W. F. Ritchie, printer, 1852.858p.-23cm. LC-E359.6 V8V82.

VIRGINIA Auditor of Public Accounts. *Pay Rolls of Militia Entitled to Land Bounty Under the Act of Congress of Sept.* 28, 1850. Richmond, Va., W. F. Ritchie, printer, 1852. 494p.-24½cm. LC-E359.5.V8V8.